Kim

  Thank you for your
continued
     support
     encouragement
     suggestions
     and
     understanding

  as we maneuvered this
little book through the
ever-changing maze of
publication.

          Blake

LOVE IN
THE WAKE OF
COVID-19©

BLAKE DANIELS PRESCOTT, MD,CM

A NOVELLA WHICH TAKES READERS THROUGH

ONE OF THE MOST CONFUSING, THREATENING,

AND POIGNANT OF TIMES, WHILE STAYING WITHIN

A HEARTBEAT OF A LOVE STORY.

In 2019, the third of three family scourges struck the globe. The first two had spread in 2003 and 2012 through 29 & 27 countries respectively and left a significant wake of death. The third, while promising a lesser mortality rate, proved to be the greatest threat.

It erupted into an official pandemic, confusing authorities with its proclivity to change, and being unpredictable in its presentation and outcome. It generated a whirlwind of rumor, denial, and lies, a misinfodemic that accompanied the pandemic and threatened to outdo it.

ISBN 978-1-09833-332-4

Come follow this disentanglement of a viral miasma.

THE CAST OF CHARACTERS

CAST: Major Characters

       Benji Sappiance

       Barbara Sappiance

       Mother, Mrs, Sappiance

       Hyo-joo Park

       Kim Sang-ook Park

       Acacia

    Minor Characters

       Tommy, Thomas Brandos

       Mandy

       Georges Bolinguet

       Pierre

       Ms Holcombe

       Puerto Rican student

       Brazilian student, Maria

       Gangly student

       Sutton

       Larry

    Alluded to

       Park parents in quarantine

       Samchon, doctor in Korea, uncle of Hyo-joo & Kim

       Acacia's father, forester

       Acacia's uncle, veterinarian

ILLUSTRATIONS

CHAPTERS

ONE   Benji and the Tree

"Hey, look at that jerk, he's huggin' a tree!"

"Where? What are ya talkin' 'bout Tommy?"

"Over there, stupid! Follow my finger. See the little turd huggin' that tree?"

"Oh, Tommy, that's Benji. You know, the one with the real good lookin' sister. He's got mental problems. You know Barbara."

"That's Barbara's brother? Nah! I don't believe it. He's puny! Hey! Let's go give him a little what for!"

"Barbara won't like that, Tommy. I thought you had the hots for her. Benji's her twin."

"Oh bull! She's twice his size. And he looks like he ain't put hair over his johnson yet."

"I didn't say they was identical. He's in a special class. My mom's an aide there. She says he's hard to reach."

"I'll show you how to reach him. Follow me."

"Oh boy, here we go."

"Hey kid, what's your name?"

"Didn't ya hear me? I asked ya for yer name. What is it?"

"C'mon Tommy. You're a big athlete. You don't need to put this kid down. It sure won't help you none with Barbara."

Tommy slammed Benji's head against the tree with the heel of his hand. "Now I got yer attention. Right? Now tell me yer name!"

Tears rolled down Benji's cheeks. Cowering, he went to the far side of the tree, using it as protection.

"C'mon Tommy, let's go play some basketball."

"Just hang on, Mandy, I need to learn this kid a thing or two. Now tell me yer screwed up name an' why you're huggin' this damn tree."

Tears worked over his cheeks as Benji inched his way to the opposite side of the tree. His head faced the tree roots but his eyes searched upward, hiding behind his eyebrows, focusing on Tommy. Finally, he spoke, "I don't like you."

"Hey, he talks! I thought he was just a fake, a little doll! But he talks! And he cries! He's just stupid!"

"I'm not stupid. I'm smart. You're stupid!"

"That does it! Now you're goin' to get a good beatin' … ya little punk. No one calls me names an' gets away with it!"

"Tommy! Look! Here comes Barbara! Oh, boy, this ain't good."

"Thomas Brandos! What do you think you're doing? Get away from my brother!"

"Hey, screw you! In fact, after I give yer retard brother here a little what for, I might just let ya have a little of me."

"You're the "retard," Thomas. You're the one who's stayed back twice and still can't manage multiplication. Benji's in a challenging class. Your challenge is to stay off cigarettes, beer, and swearing. Come on Benji, let's go home."

Grabbing her arm, and causing a book to fall from the two she was holding, Tommy leered at Barbara, drawing her close to him. "Hey, a little kiss, a little somethin' else, a little promise for more later, and then maybe I'll let up on your squirt brother."

As he pushed his body against her and tried to push her against the tree, Barbara jerked her knee up between Tommy's legs, and as he retreated, followed the knee with a sharp toe kick. Then she slammed the remaining book square in his face.

"You haven't had a chance to learn from that book yet. You'd be surprised at the powerful message it contains."

Then, she turned and added, "Mandy, I'm surprised at you. You should stop sucking up to this jerk."

"Come on, Benji. Let's go home."

TWO   Sappiance Home

"What happened to Benji? His head is all bruised."

"Well, Ma, truth be told, Benji came out of it pretty well. I think I broke Thomas Brandos's nose."

"Oh dear! Is this something I should hear about?"

"No worries, Mom. Thomas and his sycophant friend Mandy were picking on Benji. Well, it was really just Thomas. Then he grabbed me and forced himself on me; so I retaliated."

"A knee, a foot, a book," Benji added. "She protected me … and herself. She had to. He was doing bad things."

"The book got the nose. You don't want to know what the knee and foot found," Barbara clarified.

"Oh, my gracious! If only I had started teaching at Lexington Prep earlier … you both could be going there – tuition free."

"Mom, you're doing just fine and so are we. We've both been tentatively accepted in college, and Benji will get the special attention he needs there. You've done everything you can."

"We visit trees at Lexington," Benji noted. "It's better than books."

"What was going on with that big maple today, Benji?"

"I was listening. Barbara. It's a warm week, It could make a mistake and run its sap."

"You see Mom, Benji's the only one in town who listens to trees, let alone talks to them. Explaining that to someone like Thomas is like speaking Korean to him!"

"Oh, Barbara, that reminds me. The Parks are coming over for dinner. They should be here shortly. There are some family troubles back home and they need a bit of people nourishment. Something about a quarantine. Hyo-joo will explain it."

"I like Hyo-joo," Benji asserted. "She's friendly and smart. She's never mean."

"I love Hyo-joo. She's so bright and perky. Always upbeat. You're lucky to have her as a student, Mom."

"She's a fine young lady. I think she might go into medicine eventually. Well, it's very early, but she has no difficulty in any of her classes and loves the sciences."

"She's good in botany," Benji added.

"Biology with a bit of emphasis on botany since that's my passion. it's a small class but she stands out."

"She loves trees."

"Yes, Benji, she seems to have a special interest in trees just like you do."

"Is Kim coming too? You said the Parks, Mom. Is Kim Sang-ook coming?"

"Yes Barbara, Kim is coming too. I'd better get back in the kitchen."

"Barbara loves Kim." Benji stated this as if everyone knew and it was almost unnecessary to add.

"Benji! Close your trap! Kim is a wonderful, extremely bright young man. He has a wonderful sense of humor; so it's only natural that I like to be with him. He talked me into learning Taekwondo. It comes so naturally to him, I admire … well, anyone would admire a young man like him. He's fun. Still, he has some growing up to do."

A slight smile grew over Benji's face as he walked away, saying, "Barbara loves Kim."

"I'll help you in a minute, Ma. I'll just put things away and then I'll put a compress on Benji's head and some tape over his mouth."

"I'm OK. It didn't hurt that much."

"It's not over yet."

THREE   The Park Twins

"That's the door Benji. Can you get it?"

"Yes Ma."

"Hi Kim, Hi Hyo-joo."

"What happened to your forehead, Benji?"

"Oh, nothing. I got too close to a Maple."

"Benji was listening for an early sap run and a bully slammed his head against the tree. Hi Hyo-joo. Just put your coats on the rack there, Kim."

Benji added, "He went after Barbara too!"

"Oooh, that was a mistake!" Kim spoke to the wall and his coat as if they were part of the party.

"I think the bully will remember the encounter longer than Benji," Barbara explained with a smirk.

Hyo-joo handed her coat to her brother and joined Barbara. "Did he know that you are advanced in Taekwondo?"

"I tried to illustrate a toe kick, but he didn't receive it well."

"And the early sap run, Benji, did you hear any evidence of it?"

"No, Hyo-joo, not yet. The trees are smart. They will wait."

"I love your passion for trees, Benji. No one cares like you do. I'd love to take you for walks in our home area. Trees are very important to us in Korea. The pine is the tree of Korea, you know. It stays green in winter, it shows us how to go through hardship, as we do now. You would love Nami, a tiny island just filled with special trees, Benji."

"I'd like Korea. South Korea."

"Yes Benji, South Korea is very different, at least now. We, in South Korea, try to keep the past history of our country alive. We interact with our environment and appreciate it like you do. Did you know that we have scientists in South Korea who think like you do, who appreciate trees like you do? They did a study on older women in Korea and compared them when they traveled through the cities – and then again when they walked through the forests. You know what they found?"

"The women were happier in the forests. The trees liked it too."

"The women's bodies were happier. Their blood pressure was lower, their arteries were more elastic, and their lungs filled better."

"The women, their bodies, and the trees were all happier. You always make sense, Hyo-joo."

"Oh, thank you, Benji, you are so sweet. We share so much. You continue to be an inspiration for me. You know, at our home, we have beautiful gardens and lovely trees, don't we Kim?"

Yes, and at least our parents can look out on those while they are in quarantine."

"Quarantine? why are they in quarantine? Is there some terrible disease going about?" Barbara asked.

"Well it's complicated, isn't it Hyo-joo? A long story. Do we have time before dinner?"

"Ma, do we have some time before dinner?"

A voice from the kitchen replied, "Enjoy your chat. We'll eat in a half hour."

"Perhaps Hyo-joo can explain it better. I try to make light of it, and she gets upset. You know, Hyo-joo will let the rest of us relax. She will do the worrying for all of us, and she can direct all the serious talk."

"He's impossible. But he knows just as much as I do. Go ahead Kim, you tell your side. It will definitely be the lighter side."

"All right. You must excuse my simplification. I'm not the one who wants to go into medicine and loves four syllable words." Pausing, to throw a smug smile at his sister, he continued. "That bad bug that your sometime doctor-president says is going to go away is considered very scary in South Korea. We got our first case the same day you did. Yes, the very same day. The difference is, we had been burned before and were still smarting eight years later. You see, we learned. Eight years ago, we had just one person come to Korea from the Middle East and then we had an epidemic."

"That was MERS. The Middle East Respiratory Syndrome," Hyo-joo explained.

"What did I tell you? She can't resist."

Hyo-joo stuck her tongue out at him.

"As I was saying, this virus, this microbe, this MERS, taught our health authorities a lesson eight years ago; so they were prepared. When they found out that a new germ, a new Corona virus, much like the past MERS, was causing trouble in China, the KCDC was ready. Then, when that first case came to South Korea, the same day it came to the United States, our pencil pushers and our medical folks got together and traced all the people that this one person contacted; and then traced the contacts of the contacts, and then the contacts of ..."

"Kim, they understand. They also understand your prejudice for your country, and hopefully forgive your emphasis on that." Hyo-joo directed her further explanation to the Sappiance twins. "Kim's pencil pushers are our Korean Center for Disease Control, our KCDC. Evidently the contacts ran into thousands. Anyone with a significant contact was isolated, 'voluntarily' if you will, which means they were put into quarantine."

"It is voluntary isolation."

"That's what I said, Kim. Kim is not so light hearted as he appears. You see him defending his country here and not so subtly criticizing yours. He thinks you won't notice."

"Quarantine?" Benji asked.

"Yes, Benji, quarantine, as Hyo-joo says. But it could be worse. Quarantine used to mean 40 days and 40 nights. Now, they pick a number that is different depending on the bug. So they decided on two weeks. That's what our parents are facing. Two weeks of isolation, looking at their garden, being alone but being looked after as well. They have friends dropping off food. Everyone keeps a long lance distance from them, but friends look after them."

"Wow, that seems excessive, Kim. Our president says this is something like a cold. It's just going to go away. He's not making a big deal out of it. Don't you agree, Benji?"

"He's not a doctor."

"Benji and I have somewhat different political slants. I guess we are like you. Twins with different views, more like, well … please do go on. What happened with that MERS bug, Kim? That was a Corona virus as well?"

"Yes. And that is where we were burned. We still don't know the details. There was a lot of hush hush, a need for secrecy in the beginning. But what turned into an epidemic was evidently due to just one person. The government didn't want to scare people so they didn't tell them what was going on."

"Like we do now," Benji added.

"Benji, now, you hush! Go on Kim."

"It's all right Benji. I understand. Yes, we have the same problems. Not just in government, but between twins too. This MERS came to us late. It had been around for a few years before it came to South Korea. When it came, it was bad. It spread from Sunchang to Sokcho in the north; it spread even as far south as Jeju. That's our island off to the south. So it was everywhere from south to north; and from east coast to west coast. Of course our country is very small, but in spite of efforts to contain things, I think they had nearly 200 cases that were 'definite,' one hundred and eighty some odd – and two out of ten died."

"Oh my, two out of ten!" Barbara exclaimed.

"Still, South Korea did better than the global averages. Instead of two out of ten dying, as in South Korea, the global figures usually cite three to four out of ten … and sometimes more. South Korea did well with just under a 20% mortality. MERS was a real killer. We know we can't really depend upon exact figures. It's like it is here. Sometimes we get only a few teaspoons of the truth out of the bowl."

"That's not what Samchon says. He says the virus changed as it went from place to place."

"Samchon is our uncle. He's a doctor and a guiding light for my dear sister."

"He was there, in Hong Kong, for the first one!"

"True. That was the first. It was the first of these three maladies. That was SARS one. We pretty much escaped that one, but Samchon, our uncle, was unfortunate enough to be in Hong Kong where it was raging at the time. He ended up being recruited to help. We have heard that story many times. It all happened around the time that we were born, but we now know it as if we lived it. That's what uncles are for. It makes us seem, and feel, a lot older … and wiser."

"Samchon is a wonderful and brave man, Kim! One out of six died then, in Hong Kong."

"Samchon varies the story a bit. And the figures are probably not that dependable either. It was a serious germ and he was lucky to escape alive."

"So," Barbara queried, "this is a bit confusing, Kim. Your uncle, your Samchon, he was there for the first one, that was in Hong Kong. Then there was, what was it, MERS, but we have still another? These two or three microbes are all closely related, Kim?"

"Yes, all in the same bad family. They are all Corona viruses. The first one started in China, like this one. That's the first SARS or Corona virus. That's the one he fought in Hong Kong. Samchon has many names for it, none of them nice."

"What's SARS?"

"Sorry Benji, I should have explained. SARS stands for Sudden Acute Respiratory Syndrome. It's a bad disease that makes you very, very sick."

"SEVERE, acute, respiratory syndrome, Kim. You see, Barbara, he's not so smart as you think he is."

"He'll do. So the first one and this one came from China."

Samchon

"Samchon says they start in the wet markets. Excuse me for taking over dear brother. But I revere Samchon, and his explanations, more than you do. Samchon has urged Kim to go into medicine and Kim always finds an obstinate alternative. These are viruses. Samchon says they are big viruses but since they are viruses you still can't see them."

"Not unless you carry an electron microscope around with you."

"Quiet, Kim! They are little tiny balls shaped like crowns, that's why they call the family the Corona family."

"Or, it's like having a beer in Mexico."

"Kim! I gave you a chance. Just let me finish and defend Samchon. He says that they start in the wet markets where different animals are gathered – animals that would never be so close together in nature. Corona viruses love to live in bats, especially horseshoe bats. But they live in other animals too, like civets, and many, many other animals. The MERS virus, the one that came from the Middle East, loves camels. When they go from one animal to another, that's when the big trouble starts. Whether it's in a bat, a civet, a camel, a pangolin, or whatever, going from there to a human is when it really gets bad. That's when the virus jumps."

"Jumps?"

"Yes, Benji, jumps. It jumps from one kind of animal to another; and when it does it becomes especially virulent."

"She means that it gains strength and makes people a lot sicker."

"Thank you, brother. I *do* need your help! You see, he pretends not to know anything and hopes to know everything at the same time. He is impossible. But yes, he is my twin, and I give him his fair chance, Yes Kim? You see, no answer, just a nod. If he can't win, he doesn't play. Now, back to Samchon. Samchon says these Corona viruses love to change and you never know what they are going to do."

"This is the same germ, the same virus, that we have here now?"

"Yes, Barbara, or at least almost the same. It's sort of one, two, and three. Three variations. All bad. But because we had so much trouble with number two, that was MERS in South Korea, we were extra ready for number three."

"And that's why your parents are in quarantine? Are they sick?"

"No, they are fine … so far. But it can take a couple of weeks for the virus to show itself as an illness. That's why the quarantine. Samchon, our uncle stays near our parents and keeps us informed."

"So," Barbara concluded, "there is a family of viruses, this Corona family, and it has had three escapees that have been like plagues. This one now is the third. Your uncle was there for the first which was around the time we were all born, so the story of the viruses spans our lives; and the third one, the one that is causing your parents to be in quarantine, is the one that is unleashed now. Is that right?"

"You see how she listens to you Kim? You want to make sure you don't make mistakes. Barbara, you have summarized things very well, but you have ascribed a little more credit to my brother than he deserves. We hope for the best."

"As do we!" Barbara averred.

"Dinner!"

FOUR   Keep them Guessing

"That was a fine meal, Mrs, Sappiance, thank you."

"It wan't any trouble and it was a pleasure to share it with you. I'm so sorry about your family."

"Hyo-joo and I feel especially … well, being this far from home, you know, it's difficult. But you are like a second home. We thank you. We must be getting back to our dorm."

"Mom has a meeting and Benji wants to come and visit with the campus trees this weekend. Perhaps we'll run into each other, Kim."

"I hope so, Barbara. Will I see you in Taekwondo?"

"Monday afternoon! Remember how they responded when we told them we were twins?"

"Oh yes, I can't forget that one. They thought we were twins and yet were baffled by how that might be. We raised a lot of eyebrows on that one."

"Like in Taekwondo, keep them guessing."

"Two sets of twins." Mother Sappiance added. "Each individual so different. My, my, Gregor Mendel would have had a field day here." Then she retreated to her kitchen.

FIVE   Acacia

"This is a copper beech."

"Yes, Benji, I believe you're right. We should have signs on all the trees. Then the students would be more likely to learn their names. This is a very old tree. It's been here a long time."

"No, Ma. It's a youngster like me. Beeches have a very long life. This one makes it harder. It's not green. It has anthocyanins."

"You're right. I have a meeting. Can I leave you here by yourself? I don't know where Barabara ran off."

"She wants to see Kim."

"Be here when I come out. I should be about an hour."

"OK."

"What are you doing?"

"Petting the tree."

"Petting the tree?"

"Yes, to make it feel loved."

"You think trees have feelings?"

"They do."

"How can you tell?"

"Different ways. Sometimes I smell it."

"Really?"

"Yes. You like trees?"

"Yes, and no. Yes, I like trees, sometimes I love trees. I used to love trees. I come from a place where we have an immense forest. It's beautiful. But trees can be dangerous too. Up north, many people get hurt from trees."

"People hurt people more than trees hurt people."

"Well, that's an interesting observation. I believe I understand what you're implying. Anyway, back home, up north, we have lots of trees but not many great schools. That's why my father sent me here to study. My father takes me for long walks in the forest. There's so much to see there."

"Your father must be very nice."

"He's very special. He really knows the trees and their friends. He sees a scarlet tanager and says, 'Look, it's where it loves to light, on the top of that American

Sycamore.' Then he tells me about the fungi – the mushrooms we can see, and the mass of fungi that we can't … underground. That's really the important fungi."

"That's how trees talk."

"Pardon me?"

"Trees talk to each other different ways. They do it a lot using fungi."

"I think you would enjoy walking in the woods with my father."

"I like your father."

"What's your name?"

"Benji."

"My name is Acacia."

"No."

"Yes. It's a very unusual name. It's the name of a flower and a tree."

"I know. It's beautiful."

"Thank you, Benji. Do you have a last name, Benji?"

"Sappiance."

"Oh my. Are you related to Mrs. Sappiance? She's my botany teacher. Well, I really shouldn't say that, It's biology. But she teaches the botany part so well, and I enjoy botany so much, I think of her as my botany teacher."

"She's my Mom."

"Oh, how wonderful! I love your mother!"

"I love her too."

"Of course. What a treat this is for me. Do you go to school here? I don't believe I've seen you before. I'm sure I'd remember."

"I go to Damon Public. I'm in a special class. Some parts of me are ahead and some are behind."

"Well, your tree knowledge and feelings certainly aren't behind. Do you have any favorite trees?"

"I like the ones my age. I mean for trees. The beech over there, it's my age. It's about a hundred years old. But that's just a kid for beech."

"You know a lot about trees besides their feelings do you?"

"I know about you and your tree, Acacia. You have a big family. Your cousin in Africa is beautiful, like you. It has lots of pretty orange flowers like your hair and your freckles. Your face is full of beautiful flowers. Your tree has leaves that are tasty to giraffes. When a giraffe nibbles the leaves, it hurts the tree, and she sends messages to her brain in her roots, and then, the brain sends a bad toxin to the leaves to make the giraffe go away; and she also warns her sisters. That way she can stay beautiful and not hurt too much, and she helps her family. Then the giraffe has to go a long way to the next tree to find one that wasn't warned."

"It warns the other trees?"

"She sends out ethylene. It warns them. They smell the ethylene. Then they make the toxin too."

"Oh my, I'm growing fond of you, Benji."

"I'm different."

"You certainly are, in a very nice way."

"My body is slow."

"Well, your mind isn't."

"Some parts are. Some parts are very fast. Numbers are easy. I can do cubes. Do you want to hear me do cubes?"

"Cubes?"

"Yes, I'll do simple one. like 2. Like this, 2, 8, 512; you know, you just keep cubing. You can do it different ways. You can make games out of it. For instance, you can do three cubes for each number. Start with 2 and go to 3 and then to 4 and 5. So 4 would be 4, 64, and 262,144. 5 would be 5, 125, 1,953,125 … well, you get the idea. It's not fun for everyone. It's not nearly so much fun as trees but it passes time when there's nothing else – or when you want to go into yourself."

"I'm not sure I understand."

"Some people don't like me. They make fun of me. They make me turn quiet. I have to go inside then."

"Inside?"

"Inside myself. They make me want to be alone. They're mean. They're not like trees. Mean people want to hurt just to be mean. Trees hurt only if you hurt them."

"Oh my lord. Benji. You can't believe how important this meeting is."

"You make it easy for me to talk."

"Can we walk around the trees together for a little bit?"

"I would like that, Acacia. You're very pretty. You're nice, too. You understand, trees have feelings."

"Yes, Benji, and I'm beginning to understand."

sending a message downwind.

SIX
Barbara & Kim

"So, you whipped the star athlete."

"Oh, not really. First, he's not really a star, except in his own mind. He's not going to do any horseback riding soon, and his nose is a tad squashed."

"I'll have to keep you around to look after me"

"You're quite capable of caring for yourself, Kim."

"So, you've been accepted in college, Barbara."

"Yes, and no. Yes, tentatively. Everything is tentative now. But it's one we can afford. I can live at home and help Mom and Benji."

"And what about Benji?"

"He was accepted there, too. I think it's more than tentative for him. They can't get over his abilities with numbers."

"He'd be going to the same school?"

"Yes, if it all pans out. I think they're more excited about having Benji than Benji is about joining them."

"He's a fine boy, or, you know, sorry, young man. In some countries, he'd be drafted into the service next year. Sorry, I tend to put things into different context. You remember we have North Korea as our neighbor."

"Benji in the service. Now that brings up a startling image."

"You're very patient with him."

"There are times when Benji wouldn't agree. We have opposite views on many things. Politics is one. We have our innings. Just like you and Hyo-joo. And you, Kim, what are your plans for next year?"

"I'm not sure. I'm interested in a couple of universities here, but they would cost a lot and Samchon would like me to attend university at home. He keeps trying to push me."

"And you resist."

"Not really so much. I don't know what I want to do. Not yet, anyway. I don't like being away from you."

"What about Canada? Have you thought about going back there? That's where you and Hyo-joo honed your English so well. They have a very different attitude toward the coronavirus – at least I think they do – from what little I understand. Mother says that the politicians seem to be of one mind and even compliment each other on how this viral plague is not a political issue. She says liberals and conservatives forget their party lines when it comes to the coronavirus. They might be more receptive to your returning for further schooling."

"True, and Hyo-joo and I have thought about it … and talked a lot about it. Samchon says the Canadian experience was much like ours in South Korea. Just as Korea was burned and scarred by only one person who caused the epidemic of MERS in Korea, so Canada had a similar experience with the first SARS back in 2003. Just as that one person who came from Saudi Arabia caused the Korean epidemic and the loss of so many lives, so did just one person coming from Hong Kong cause terrible suffering in Canada. That's why they are doing so well now. It's unreal how one person can cause so much difficulty."

"I don't understand. What happened?"

"Well, SARS-One, the first of the really bad coronaviruses – the one where Samchon helped by going to Hong Kong treating those who were so terribly ill – that SARS-One had quieted down, and people started to feel safe. They thought it was over … or soon would be over. Samchon remembers it like it was yesterday. That was in 2002 to 2003. We were all infants. Samchon was finally getting some rest with Hong Kong showing some relief. He said that they still had active cases but not like it had been. That's when one person, a person who was visiting Hong Kong, left to return home to Toronto."

"It was 2003 and it was a Canadian woman who returned to Toronto from her visit to Hong Kong. She felt well but, unfortunately, she had been exposed to SARS-One. She went to her home in Toronto. Then, she became ill, very ill. So, as the story goes, she and her son went to the emergency room at a hospital in Toronto and sat for hours in a crowded waiting room. That wait, that sitting with others for so long in close quarters, that was a serious problem. That mother, as Samchon says, was the index case, the one that caused the infection to spread – eventually to 375 further cases, nearly half of whom were health care workers. Forty four people died. This was the second wave of SARS-One."

"The World Health Organization, responded with an advisory quarantine on Toronto that eventually resulted in over a billion dollar loss for the province of Ontario. So Canada learned her lesson from that incident in 2003 to 2004. They were ready, just like we in South Korea were ready. Two countries, two lessons, and two sister-like responses."

"I had no idea."

"Yes, if I don't return to our home in Korea, nothing would please Samchon more than my going to Canada."

"Then you plan on going to Canada?"

"No."

"You made many friends there. You liked the people."

"Yes, but I would prefer to stay in the States."

"You told me you had a girlfriend, a steady girlfriend when you were in Canada."

There was a pause, Kim looked away from Barbara, then he smirked and said, "I said that just to make you jealous."

"Oh, Kim, what am I to do with you?"

"You could … let's see, you could be warmer, closer, and … more inviting, less serious, and …"

"You should be a bit more serious, Kim."

"I could take an extra year; not here at Lexington – unless they would let me. Perhaps another school nearby. A postgrad year. It would give me time to decide. More time to think …"

"More time to play, more time to delay, more excuses, Kim?"

"True, you see … well, as we both know, you see too much. But, if I did that, I'd be learning just as I would anywhere else, and I'd be here."

"And you wouldn't have to work so hard."

"We could be close."

"I'd better not say anything. You should do what is right for you. You know how I feel, Kim. What about Hyo-joo?"

"Well, she can take an accelerated course back home. It would save her a year and she could go on to medical school."

"What if she changes her mind?"

"I don't think that's going to happen."

"Maybe you should just tell Samchon that Hyo-joo is really a boy in disguise."

"He's really proud of her. I think he just doesn't want to see me go off on some derelict path."

"Derelict?"

"He wants me to be focused, too focused. I do need a little time to play. You grow up only once, and once you've grown up, you have to be … well, too immersed. There's lots of time."

Barbara   Prepares

SEVEN   The Faucet Opens for Benji

You could hear the rain pounding on the panes, demanding an entrance and occluding a view of its outside agitation. Preceding it was a gray day, drizzling discomfort, drizzling steadily for hours; together, the drizzle and the rain, promised to melt what snow was left, offering a premature change in seasons.

In deference to Benji's feelings and preference, they collected and burned only standing dead wood for their small, soapstone stove – their source of living room heat. On dank, dark days like this one, the stove drew the family together, adding another personality to the room, and inviting a different tone of conversation. Piano music streamed in from the next room, familiar melodies punctuated by an occasional dissonance and grunt of words better forgotten.

"Mom should practice more."

"Or maybe less, Benji."

"She loves music."

"That's what makes her swear."

"She misses Dad."

"We all miss Dad, Benji."

"It's not fair."

"You're right about that one, Benji.

"I met a very nice girl."

"You're kidding."

"No, I'm not. She's very nice."

"That's not … never mind. Tell me about her. I'm all ears."

"Her name is Acacia, like the flower, like the tree. She goes to Mom's school. I met her when you went to visit Kim."

"Don't stop there, Benji. Tell me more."

"She's very smart and very pretty. Her face is filled with flowers that match her hair."

"Her face is filled with flowers! Explain a little more?"

"She has freckles."

"Oh, of course."

"She wanted to walk with the trees. I told her cubes but she liked trees better."

"Yes, do go on."

"Her father lives in the woods. He taught her about trees. She knew all the trees we talked to. She didn't know what the Acacia tree does when it hurts. I told her. She liked that story."

"That's lovely, Benji."

"She wants to visit again. She has a bad leg. Or maybe both legs are a little bad. She doesn't move fast. Mom says she's special. She's advanced."

"Oh my, Benji, this sounds serious."

"She's serious but she's fun. She knows all about botany and biology. She's writing a paper on viruses. Viruses hurt plants just like they do animals."

"Acacia sounds like a very special person. I can't wait to meet her."

"She's short, like me. She has a special uncle just like Kim and Hyo-joo. He's a doctor but he's a doctor for cows and pigs."

"He's a veterinarian?"

"Yes. He gave her the idea for the virus paper. Because she's advanced, she has to write a paper. She plays chess too."

"It sounds like you two had a long conversation."

"It was mostly about trees. She loves trees like I do. She explained about different mangroves and how they work with salt water. They're pioneers. They're pioneers on the shore." Benji paused and smiled. "She's funny too."

"She's funny?"

"Yes, she asked me if I knew what the record was for the hundred yard dash in a red mangrove swamp."

"A hundred yard dash through mangroves? They've got all those twisted roots. You can hardly move through them. You remember when we visited Andros? You remember the red mangroves there? I'm sorry, Benji, she may have been mistaken."

"She wasn't. She made a joke. The hundred yard dash record through the red mangroves, that was a joke."

"And the answer, the joke, was?"

"That's what makes it funny. The answer was two days."

"Did you laugh?"

"I giggled for a long time. She's very pretty, and she's really nice. She's been to the Amazon."

"Really!"

"Yes, and she told me how different the trees are there. It's a rain forest – thick with trees but the soil is skinny, so the trees need extra help to stay up. Many have

buttresses – like old churches; they have extra little trunks, something like the mangroves but they don't do it for air and getting rid of salt, they do it to stand up in the thin soil. They stand up like churches in the rain forests. It's a place where you can pray."

"Oh Benji, this is beginning to sound very serious."

"She told me more about the rain forests. There are lots of animals that eat the trees, especially insects.The trees are almost all different and they live very close together. They show how you can be different and still be part of a big family. The trees make lots of poisons to keep from being eaten, but when a tree falls and makes an opening, an opening to the sunshine, the neighbors stop making the poisons and put all their energy into growing; they try to fill the opening. They have to grow fast and put up with being hurt by insects eating them. Later they make poisons again. They measure everything by hectares there."

"Wow, Benji. I haven't heard you go on like this. Acacia really made an impression on you."

"Her father is a forest expert. He's traveled all over the world. He took her too. He lives with trees. He knows about the medicines in the trees too."

The music stopped with a dissonant bang and a few words, "Those are too many damn flats!"

"What are you two up to?"

"Benji has been telling me about Acacia! I've never heard him go on like this."

"Oh yes, Acacia is a delightful woman. She's small, and looks very young, but she's a woman. Like you and Benji, she's older, but young. You and Benji are older than most in your class. That was my fault. When your father died. Well, I'm not going into that again. It all turned out well. I think Acacia has yet another year on you. She was kept out of conventional schooling for awhile, just like you were. I'm not sure what her delays were for. She's taking a post grad year now. For her it's more of a concentration on a few areas. I think she's trying to decide what her next path might be. I'm really fortunate to have her in my biology class. She teaches me as much as I teach her."

"She certainly has made an impression on Benji."

"Well, if truth be told, I think he made an impression on her as well.

EIGHT   SARS, MERS, & COVID;
The Familia Corona

Near the shores of southern New England, there was little hint of the snow pack up north, yet there was talk here, as there was elsewhere, of filling the northern chalets with the adolescents and young adults bestrewn over the country; indeed, this might be necessary rather than an option. This was considered to be an exceptional suggestion, but this was an exceptional and, indeed, singular time. There was no pattern for people to follow. All this was because of the virus.

The virus was a 'lead in' to each conversation, a back stage player who loomed over stage front, a concern and imminent threat to pockets of our country, an ongoing menace in some areas of the world, a threat to spread both locally and distantly, and a ripe source for conjecture since so little was known about it.

The corona virus had spread into the West Coast of the States. There was some talk of isolating students there, of reverting to media teaching, and doing mandatory testing of students and faculty for the virus. The testing got little heed since testing measures were already noted to be in short supply, dearly needed in the hospital setting, and – reputed as unreliable. Preventative measures, like wearing a surgical mask, were pushed by many but governmental and authoritarian advice indicated they might be relatively useless; in any case, they were needed and used by those confronting active cases and were also in very short supply. There was no singular voice; there was only a spectrum of rumor. One of those rumors was that some schools might suspend class – particularly those in hot bed areas. This could necessitate sending students from prep schools and colleges back home. It was said that they would pose a risk to those whom they would contact on coming home, especially the old and the infirm. So this is why folks were talking about using the ski chalets as a natural retreat for this healthier, more resistant, arguably risky, and possibly less compliant segment of society.

Advice had no common denominator. People were advised to stay in, unless they were advised to go out, they were advised to wear a mask, unless they were advised not to wear a mask, they were advised to go to work, unless they were advised not to go to work, they were advised to stay apart unless they needed to be together. People were told the virus would go away in the warmer weather, but it was starting to thrive in the southern hemisphere where it was warm. There was no strident voice with a clear message. The ridiculous overrode the sensible and scientific.

Rumors were rife. Celebrities became authorities on viral nuances. Government officials offered almost every imaginable, varying view. This was nothing and it was going to go away on its own. This was serious and warranted strict quarantine, This wan't happening. This was devastating and was the fault of … and then there would be a wide choice of what and whom to blame.

There was no limit to the social media offerings and no shortage of exaggerated claims and cures. Gargling with warm salt water would prevent it, a temperature in the low 90s – below human body temperature – would kill the virus, swallowing would kill the virus once hitting the stomach acid, garlic would both prevent and cure the problem (as well as keeping vampires away).

The virus acquired different names: Corona virus, novel Corona virus, SARS Corona Virus, the SARS part indicating Severe Acute Respiratory Syndrome, but then there had been two other SARS, so this was either number three – or, it could be number two. If you didn't count the second one as a SARS – since it was called MERS, meaning Middle East Respiratory Syndrome, this was only number two. Confusing. The first SARS was now referred to as SARS Cov-1, and was getting further attention in its now nearly 18 year old wake. This present one was being called SARS Cov-2 but that held the tongue in play a tad extensively.

MERS, too, was getting a closer second look, but generally retained its original name, not succumbing to the further and, arguably, more appropriate MERS-CoV identification as a Corona virus. Its origin and attachment to the Middle East, particularly the Arabian peninsula and neighboring Jordan, was its major moniker. Indeed, since the largest outbreak of MERS outside of the Arabian peninsula was in South Korea, and that was the result of only a single infected traveler returning from Saudi Arabia, the Middle East was married to the malady, along with its purported reservoir of camels. MERS was re-examined to shed light on the present Coronavirus problem, especially since MERS seemed to almost go away on its own, slowly slipping away after having wreaked its havoc some 5 to 8 years previously.

Long lasting and serious aftereffects of both SARS-Cov-1 and MERS were being unearthed. Long lasting and some permanent neurological complications associated with those two afflictions were now seen in a different light since they might well apply to the current scourge.

This latest corona virus, this present epidemic, evidently started in December of 2019, in the Wuhan area of China. Was it a Wuhan virus? Might it be a Chinese plague like the Spanish flu? Shortening the longer tongue twisters, most people settled on calling this third one simply COVID-19. This appellation covered COrona VIrus Disease and indicated it to have been first noticed in 2019; case closed. It was one of those three Corona viruses causing severe disease. And, like its sisters, this COVID-19 wasn't just a respiratory problem, it could be a GI problem, or a heart problem, or a skin problem, or a blood vessel problem.

There were still other corona viruses that affected man, but these caused illnesses akin to colds; so only the big three were counted. Apparently no one paid attention to the Corona family members that did so much in so similar a fashion to animals other than man. One had resulted in the killing of three million pigs in one year. No one talked about that, but the pigs probably remember it well.

Little was certain. There was a lack of international agreement as to the definitive qualities of the virus and there was a minimum of international cooperation. Efforts to share experience, share testing, and share personal protective equipment, or PPE, too often went wanting, while rumors continued to balloon and spread. There seemed to be an overriding dictum not to share knowledge but to spread blame. Countries had individual problems since they acted individually. States were to fend for themselves. Blame was left to land wherever and whenever the wheel and the music stopped.

Practically every conversation somehow invited COVID-19 into it. Everyone became an authority. Multitudes made statements asserted as facts, but with uncertain foundations, The virus started in the wet markets in Wuhan, China. The Corona virus family has many reservoirs, in a wide variety of animals. Bats are a major reservoir. In wet markets animals are brought into unnatural proximity; therefore, this is a natural place for the virus to jump and spread. No, it didn't come from the wet markets, it came from a laboratory in Wuhan where they were doing research; this was an escapee. It started in a seafood market in Wuhan. No, this was a chemical weapon developed by the Chinese. The stories of illness and death in China are all exaggerations; this was unleashed purposefully. You could choose your story and find no difficulty in finding adherents.

Once the conversation started, the two sister scourges, SARS -1 and MERS soon became attendees. The death toll from each of those two previous Coronas was generally cited as 20 to 30%, an impressive and frightening figure. COVID-19 was being noted as closer to 6 or 7%, but figures varied as much as did the stories of the origin or presentation of the illness. There was little that was certain, much that was controversial, little that was confirmed, and much that was charged with emotion rather than erudition.

As to the two preceding Corona viruses, these two sisters, once unleashed, spread their wrath over a half dozen countries and lasted for two to three years. And then they virtually disappeared. No treatment, at least none that reliably killed the virus, no vaccine, at least none for humans, became available. Still these two preceding menaces disappeared on their own. Wny? How? No one knew. Would this present virus, this COVID-19 act like a member from the past? Would it be different? What was predictable? Was this an epidemic? Could this be a pandemic?

A flood of statements was constantly in the process of being fact checked; nonetheless, the errors, misunderstandings, misleading assertions, and purposely prejudicial seductions had left their imprint and, indeed, only a determined few waited to review subsequent factual analyses.

Many perpetuated the initial rumors. Depending upon how the rumor fit with personal bias and personality, proselytes emerged to foster a variety of causes.

NINE   Local Effects

This was a time of uncertainty, concern, and understandable fear. The Sappiance family was no exception. The public high school as yet had no restriction imposed due to the virus; people gathered as before. Classes met as usual, athletic events were unchanged, and the auditorium periodically filled.

Athletics at Damon High were revered by parents. It was one of the areas where the school stood out. It also kept the students in a safe haven when parents were at work.

Many of the parents of the public school students insisted that the threat of this virus was overblown and the current response was an overreaction. They further insisted that if classes were to be modified or suspended, the school should provide oversight and safe gathering places, particularly for the younger students. The parents could not afford to give up their jobs to supervise, let alone teach, children. Strong feelings from parents were echoed by offspring, dividing the school into factions.

Tommy and Mandy thought this was all a hoax. Tommy said he'd start a bonfire on the baseball diamond if they canceled any of his games. He boasted how no virus could stop *him*. He'd go catch it just to prove it! Tommy, himself, started a quip which he proudly repeated countless times.

"It's like chicken pox. You get it and you get over it. Only chickens don't get it." Somehow, Tommy developed a small but steady cadre of students who touted and shouted his mantra. They taunted, jeered, humiliated, and challenged their fellow students.

"You're with us or you're chickens." That was Tommy's opening statement, and, too often, followed by a physical punctuation mark. And where that didn't seem to be enough, he'd have his crew join him in "pantsing" people. This was very effective in reducing opposing views.

Barbara gave advice to Benji. "Stay away from Tommy's gang. And, remember, Benji, we go home together."

Thanks to the virus, Tommy was becoming more of a hero at Damon Public – or, in the eyes of an apparent minority, an anti-hero.

It was rather different at Lexington Prep. There was no gang demanding a singular point of view, but there was no shortage of opinion … or deep concern. And, there was no curtailment of expression of opinion. As yet, there was no constraint of gathering, no report of nearby illness or threat of spread within the school, but there was such a varied student body from widely spread parts of the world, that a disparate and dramatic playing of contrapuntal themes filled the campus each day.

Relatives were in hospital in Britain and France, the virus was not acknowledged in Brazil, New Zealand showed the world how to deal with this, Italy was suffering and crying for help, Singapore was exemplary, Hong Kong was not representative of China, Senegal requested their example be followed, Washington State was in trouble – trouble reflected by the tears of students away from that home, New York City was indicative of congestion and a thermometer for others to measure. The virus had struck in many places where the students had left heartbeats.

Lexington offered an intersection of concerns, apprehensions, angst, and consternation. The traffic was running amok.

The faculty at Lexington decided that a sound way of allowing the student body to ventilate, learn, and find some reassurance, would be a discussion – or perhaps a debate – or better, an elucidation demonstrating mutual support. This could be particularly helpful for those with families in hot zones; it would use information, empathy, and understanding as a glue to bring the school together in this most fractured time. Eight students volunteered to participate. Hyo-joo was one and Acacia was another.

No, the virus had not significantly invaded home territory of the Sappiance family, but concern and rumors had come like scud clouds – and had rained heavily on all with ears. Indeed, rumors had prevailed as a premonitory epidemic which needed to be dispelled as badly as did COVID-19.

TEN   Preparatory Hugs & Jabs

"It's so nice to have you over to our house, Acacia."

"Well, Mrs Sappiance, if truth be told, this is one of the most meaningful afternoons I've had this year. Being able to compare preparations for the virus discussion with Hyo-joo, having Benji by my side as a coach, you being here … well, that is more than I could ask for. But then, to have Barbara as well! She's amazing. I'm so glad to meet her. She's truly a person beyond her years and so wise, so knowledgeable, so understanding of Benji. You are blessed to have a daughter like her, Mrs Sappiance."

"Well, I'll let you all get back to work. I'll rustle something up for dinner. Are you looking at the virus from the standpoint of plants, Acacia?"

"No, Mrs Sappiance, I have an uncle who is a veterinarian. He has been schooling me in the Corona family. It's fascinating. I truly think it's an area that hasn't been touched by most people. Well, in any case, I do hope that I can make it as interesting for the students listening as it has been for me. The vets even had a vaccine."

"Really! I guess we should listen more closely to our veterinarian experts."

"It's complicated, but my uncle is like Hyo-joo's uncle. He is dedicated and loves his work. He makes it all seem so much simpler. He loves to share his enthusiasm. That means it's hard for him to stop once he starts. It doesn't matter whether he's on the phone or hiding in an email. In fact, I usually put his emails to one side so that I can absorb them better – waiting until after I've done my assigned homework."

"Fascinating. Well, I shall be soaking in all your ideas as they come into the kitchen. In this small house, ideas don't escape very far."

"I really like your mother," Acacia uttered automatically as she turned to face Benji and Barbara.

"We like her, too," Benji replied.

Barbara brought Acacia back into the midst of the discussion with, "You were talking about the ancient history of the Corona family."

"Oh yes, that was really an aside. they have been around so long. Thousands of years. Why it was in the time of the Greeks some two or three thousand years ago that they divided into the families of alpha, beta, gamma, and delta – just as we know them today."

"Viruses knew Greek." Benji asserted.

"Oh Benji, Acacia brings out your sense of humor!" Barbara noted, and then turned to Acacia. asking, "Are those four types important?"

"Actually, yes, in a simple way. Humans are infected by both alpha and beta, but beta are the especially bad ones. That's where we find the SARS and MERS. Still, alpha has been really bad for pigs and pigs are closely related to humans."

"I knew it!" Kim couldn't restrain himself. "I've met a few who are *very* closely related!"

"Kim, please, dear brother, allow Acacia to explain."

"It's OK, Kim, I enjoy your humor. A little humor will help us in getting things across in our presentations. As to the pigs, the Greek pigs, if Benji has his way, the alphas have really been bad; four of the alphas have been especially severe in causing disease and death in pigs; it's the nemesis to pigs like beta has been to humans. The point here is that the darn viruses just keep changing and threatening to be worse. We have to look at the whole family to learn. For example, with one of the alphas, they found that piglets shed the virus in their stools and that the virus was aerosolized when these piglets had forceful diarrhea; the amazing part was that they found those aerosolized viral particles spread up to ten miles!"

Kim naturally picked up here, "Talk about the disadvantage of being downwind! So if a person is similarly sick with diarrhea, and they go into the common bathroom …"

"Yes, Kim, dear, dear, brother. We get the point." Then, directing her attention back to Acacia, Hyo-joo continued, "So, if we study the family, if we know what it has done and likes to do to pigs, cows, or others, we see what it may want to do to us."

"True. You see, as my uncle points out, this family has been well known in veterinary circles for a long time. The Corona family is known for unfortunate family traits."

"And," announced from the side by Kim, "those traits, those peculiarities, …"

"Enough, Kim!. Please Acacia, go on. Excuse Kim. My brother, even though not volunteering for the debate, is determined to conduct the preparation. You're fortunate in not having had a twin. Do go on, Acacia. This helps me with my presentation as well."

"Well, simply put, but bluntly, like my uncle would put it, the Corona family of viruses has great potential for devastating effect, and has done it. Three million pigs died one year due to one outbreak. Cows have been repeatedly, horribly afflicted, and with impressive death tolls. Once established, the virus keeps its household in a species and has a reservoir for further transmission. The gut and the respiratory tract have been favorite sites. Even after getting better, the animals have been re-infected! Can you imagine that? Sometimes it seems impossible to eradicate the virus from an animal. It can keep passing it on through its stool."

"How does it go from one cow to another through the stool?" Hyo-joo was puzzled "Is it aerosolized like with the piglets?"

"My uncle says that just as when a cow urinates and splashes the urine on a concrete floor, it aerosolizes and then it's breathed in and … well then it"s on its way to the next victim. This happens with other germs like the one cows give to milk maids. But that one is a spirochete and much bigger. This is a virus; tiny and should aerosolize all the easier. So, when the cow passes a stool, especially when it's explosive with cramps and gas, some goes into the air, it aerosolizes, and then another animal or human breathes it in …"

"You see!" said Hyo-joo, "It's what was said by Samchon. Samchon is right again! It's different from other viruses. You remember his story about the poorly ventilated bathrooms in the apartment buildings in China? That's how they had the big spread in the beginning in Wuhan! The virus is in the air! And, the same point he makes! It's in the lung and the gut. What other virus does this?"

"Flu doesn't."

"You're right, Benji. Flu causes respiratory problems. When you have vomiting or diarrhea, that's not flu, it's grippe or some other kind of illness!" Hyo-joo averred.

"And you were saying how this virus wants to change, Hyo-joo. Just as your uncle tells you that it is happening now like it did in Hong Kong, and as it did later with MERS, my uncle said the same thing about it when trying to deal with the complications with cattle. Every time it would go through a few animals, you would see a new aspect, usually something worse. Going through animals, that is its 'passage,' this has been its way of changing. It has a great desire to get stronger, more virulent."

"You had said something before, something about combining viruses, Acacia."

"Oh, yes, Hyo-joo, that's another way the virus makes big changes. When infected with more than one, the viruses break down and then recombine, and then you have a chance for a super virulent form."

Barbara interjected, "I'm confused. More than one infection at the same time? This must be rare. This is just in pigs and cows and … whatever?"

"Actually, I think one is common in children – or at least infants; it causes bad diarrhea. In fact, I think we have a vaccine that is given to infants for it." Acacia thought for a moment. "It's called rotavirus."

Kim couldn't resist adding, "Rotarooter causes diarrhea, how surprising!"

"Brother Kim, you are trying my patience! Continue Acacia."

Acacia looked at Kim and smilingly said, "I appreciate that you are listening, Kim. If I keep your interest, then perhaps I can do the same for others."

"You see, dear sister, I am appreciated."

Hyo-joo made a face at Kim, turned to Acacia, and advised, "Don't encourage him, Acacia. He pretends to be the fool. It's a game for him. Now you said that this coronavirus family loves to change. It does it as it passes from one animal to the next and it does it when it combines with its nefarious friends, one of those being the rotavirus, not rotarooter."

"Right, Hyo-joo, right on. There's the rotavirus and another one that causes diarrhea that is closely related to the coronavirus, in fact, it even looks like a coronavirus, called torovirus. These two are especially likely to breakdown and recombine with the coronaviruses and cause extra trouble."

"So," summarized Hyo-joo, "Two gut viruses, one that we give vaccines to infants to try to prevent, one very closely related to coronaviruses, rota and toro, are special examples of those that recombine with coronaviruses and when they do, you can end up with a super corona."

Kim glanced over to Benji and half whispered, "My sister is trying to get a head start on med school."

Ignoring her brother, Hyo-joo persisted, "Yes, Acacia, but Samchon says that the Coronas look for certain tissues, particular organs; he says there is a common denominator." Then she glanced at her brother and added, "Like knowing that if there is dessert hanging around, there's one person who can be counted on to sneak it away and pretend it never happened. The common denominator for the virus, the corona family, is it that they like lungs and the gut? You say we see the same with the cattle and the pigs. Samchon says the virus looks for receptors and these are present not just in the gut and the lungs, but in the heart, the throat, and the blood vessels."

"My sister listens to Samchon instead of going to church."

"Quiet, Kim! You revere what he says just as much as I do. You just pretend that you don't in order to shirk responsibility."

"Ooh, winning kick from sister! OK, tell Acacia about your 4 H club. Sorry, 5 H club. That's something that even I can understand, Hyo-joo. I was explaining that to Barbara and she thought it was a real winner for the discussion, didn't you Barbara?"

"Yes, Kim. That is a winner. Not the kick, the H's. How does it go again, Hyo-joo?"

"It's my way of explaining viruses to myself." Hyo-joo apologized. "They are such simple little organisms and can't live on their own. They need another being, a cell to live in; otherwise they don't survive. They need to find some place where they can take over a cell and make it work for them. But they don't have a way of getting to good real estate, good tissue, on their own. And they need to take an easy way to get there. That's how I came up with the 5H club for the viruses and put it as a headline for the Coronas."

"Go on, Hyo-joo," Barbara added. Tell us how you might present it in the debate – or whatever this ends up being."

"OK. Let's see. Viruses can't do much of anything by themselves. They lie around, hoping to survive long enough to get a ride. They have to Hitch Hike. They don't have their own car or motorcycle. So, someone touches an area where a person has coughed and has left the virus. Now a hand picks it up. The virus was Hitch Hiking and you just picked it up to give it a ride. But it won't do any harm on your hand. It needs a Highway to go where it can get to prime real estate and take over a Home. You put your hand to your face, your mouth, your nose, or your eye, and now the virus is on a Highway and can get to the kind of cell that it can take over, like those in the upper and lower respiratory tract. It finally finds a cell it likes. It Hijacks that cell. The cell doesn't do its own job anymore. It just does the bidding of the virus. The bidding is replicate, replicate, replicate. Just do nothing but make more little viruses. The cell is turned into a virus making factory. So, the virus Hitch Hikes, finds a Highway, reaches a Home cell, and then it Hijacks the Home cell. It's the 5H club."

"I love it!" Barbara asserted.

You could stress what Samchon said about the mutants."

"I think I do that, Kim, when I talk about the virus changing all the time. It gets stronger or weaker, it wants different Homes, different tissues, and, well, as it changes what it does, the result will change too. In the lung you cough, in the gut, you vomit. Always changing. Always different. Sometimes diarrhea, sometimes cough, sometimes hardly sick, sometimes very sick."

"But remember what Samchon wrote in his last email. The one in China is not the same as the one in Korea. The one in Europe is different. The one in the States is like the one in Europe. It helps to explain why some people are so sick and some aren't."

"Yes, Kim we know. No need to show off. It's not just the virus, Kim. Some people are weaker, like jeungjo halmeoni." Then Hyo-joo explained to others, "She is our mother's grandmother."

Barbara took charge of the situation and suggested, "It looks like you're both off to an excellent start. Perhaps we should leave you to revamping things on your own. Whatever you decide to do, you have the knowledge. I am very impressed with how much you've learned. You've certainly taught me a good deal in no time at all."

"You see, Kim," Hyo-joo added, "how courteous she is? You don't know how lucky you are."

ELEVEN   Lexington & the Globe

The Lexington campus was now a cacophony of conversations. Accents tinged stories which crisscrossed and converged, some reiterating disturbing tales from home, others reflecting home concern for the students, for their anticipated travel, for their returning home, or … for their not being able to return home. The resounding theme behind much of this was, naturally, the virus.

Only a few days after South Korea and the United States experienced their first case of this plague, it made its presence in Europe. Each country had its own story and its own way of dealing with the virus. Passengers returning from the hotbed of Wuhan China flew back to the the United States; they were screened for fever in Alaska and then again, when landing in California; they were to undergo observation for three days before being considered safe. Americans had been told that the risk was low by the authorities toward the end of January while WHO, the World Health Organization, declared the coronavirus outbreak to be a "public health emergency of international concern." Then the US reported its first recognized case of person to person transmission and the Trump administration declared the coronavirus outbreak to be a public health emergency; the administration set quarantines on Americans recently returning from certain parts of China and initiated a ban on foreign nationals who had been in China in the previous 14 days. At that point, statistics were unreliable, especially from China where it was said that they reported only the hospitalized cases. Nonetheless, the only reported deaths due to the virus at that time were from China. It was said that there had been some 12,000 cases and 250 deaths. As February came in, those were the only deaths that were "certain."

Then, with the advent of February in a bissextile year, promising an extra day for the virus to wreak havoc, the story started to change. The virus had spread to the Phillipines and taken a life there. And, as the virus spread, so did stories. There was the story of a "whistleblower" doctor in China who had warned other doctors of the seriousness of the disease; he died, succumbing to the very disease himself.

In mid February, WHO officially tagged this new virus with the appellation of COVID-19.

Toward the end of that month, Italy locked down, closing schools, businesses, and restaurants. Italian students in Lexington feared not being able to return home or, if able to return, not being able to come back – to resume schooling in the States.

At the end of February, the Vice President in the United States was designated to lead a task force to battle COVID-19. Our testing in the States was admitted as flawed, and rather than accept testing as done by other countries, companies in the US were invited to attack and correct this problem. The FDA facilitated this by altering the rules for adoption of new testing technologies.

And then, and now, we were in March. This was a month of turmoil. COVID-19 was exploding in Italy. Reports from home superseded official documents. Everyone looked for definitive information; everyone feared reading the next email or opening the next letter from home. No place seemed secure; no place was safe. Rumors were rife and knowledge was wanting. Authoritative information was often conflicting.

The European Center for Disease Contol, The ECDC, sent out a statement at the start of March, while holding on to one of the older names, ie, novel corona virus, indicating that the upcoming risk for sustained spread of the virus throughout Europe and the UK was moderate to high. They reported that of the then recognized nearly 90,000 cases globally, only just over 2000 were in the official EU/EEA/UK count. But the death count had also started, and it, too, was rising.

Italy, Spain, and France had received viral sucker punches, the suffering was mounting each day, and Germany was now indicating a similar pattern. Each of these countries was represented by members of the student body at Lexington. Even the UK, another wellspring for Lexington, was sending messages from home which, while trying to reassure, were filled with concern and alluded to the possibility of worse.

Hyo-joo and Kim received regular communications from parents, other relatives, and friends. Samchon, while indicating he was busy, was faithful in keeping the twins up to date. Samchon had a compelling story to relate. It was about a single person and what only one person could do. In this case, it was not good.

The story referred to one woman, a sick woman, a woman, who attended a religious ceremony in Daegu, a ceremony where there were some thousand worshippers, all probably praying to avoid being struck by the virus. So what seemed to have been an ideal response to the first case in January, now was ruined, approximately a month later, purportedly by this one woman. She had been infected with the virus, she managed to change the religious gathering of the Church of Jesus into an overrunning petri dish, spreading devastation in every direction. All the caution previously taken was crushed.

As February closed in South Korea, the number of cases exploded and that country was second only to China in its tally for being struck. Samchon was equally struck. On the one hand, he was frightened, disheartened, disappointed, and reluctant to tell the story to Hyo-joo and Kim. On the other, he was able to reassure them. The family was well. The attendees, the worshipers, and their contacts were being identified and notified; they were to isolate, to prevent further spread; they were to self quarantine. There was a battle between the government and this religious group. The government was prevailing. Samchon felt this would be effective in snuffing this unfortunate match.

So it was, depending upon from whence they came, so came the news. Little was greatly reassuring; all was attached with love, none indicated any assurance as to the future.

This news, coming from home, added punctuation marks and tears to the cacophony of conversations. Emotion soaked the words, concern interrupted study patterns, and students found similar problems in dissimilar ethnicities; students supported one another as not in the past. They looked forward to the debate, discussion, and disentanglement of the virus that was to occur in short of a fortnight. Everyone looked for clarity and support. Everyone hoped that the need for this would pass.

TWELVE   Pierre

"Oh, hi Benji. I thought you'd be in school. Did they close it down due to the viral scare?"

"No, Acacia. I'm playing hooky!"

"Benji, how naughty!"

"Barbara's playing hooky too! She's naughty too. She's with Kim."

"Oh, I see. Yes that does sound naughty. Does your mother know?"

Benji held his finger up to his lips.

"Oh dear! By the smirk on your face, I expect that you're enjoying your truancy."

" I came to visit the trees. I hoped I'd see you."

"Well, I have a class in five minutes, but if you can be here after that, I'd love to see you."

"I'll be here."

Acacia reached over and gave Benji a kiss on the cheek, turned quickly, and while quickly limping off, shouted, "Later!"

Benji's face changed. His eyes opened wide, a scarlet hue captured his skin, and, while his mouth remained almost closed, a grin took over the real estate of his lower countenance. No one to hear, but he uttered again, "I'll be here." Then he started to stroll through the trees.

Sitting, sitting forward with his head and hands on his raised knees, sitting alone under a single and most unusual tree, sat a hidden face with tears seeping between the fingers. Benji walked over and cautiously approached, but there was no response except a quiet sobbing coming from between the fingers. Benji looked up at the tree, then at the top of the boy's head, then back at the tree. Then he sat down. He sat not quite an arm's length from the boy. He reached out and slowly, softly, gradually placed his palm on the shoulder of the boy.

The boy's head turned as he raised it and dropped his arms to one side, all done slowly, as had Benji, as if choreographed in andante. His right hand held some papers, crumpled, but held most firmly. He stared at Benji, and then looked down at the papers. He spoke from his throat. "Eet is the baad news." He spoke slowly and hesitatingly, his words suffocated with feeling.

"Ma mère, she send the email. I cannot stay eenside. I copy the email and bring it 'ere – to read again … and again. I need the spaace. I need the air. Il faut

…I need the air like mon père … sorry … my father, 'ee is een 'ospitaal. 'ee is very ill. 'ee cannot talk. A machine breathes for 'eem. No air is enough for 'eem. Eet is the very baad news."

Benji didn't move. He just stared at the boy. He kept his hand on his shoulder.

"'ee has the verus. The baad one! They said … they thought … they thought he had mal de coeur, pain from the heart … douleur cardiaque! 'ee had the beeg pressure on his chest. 'ee could not breathe. But 'ee had the cough too. 'ee was so weak. 'ee could not walk. Only the crawl, 'ee crawl to the toilette. And the feaaver. 'ee thought, peut etre, eet is the flu. Then up with the eensides. 'ee vom-eet. And from the other end too. Everything at once. Then the 'ospitaal. Worse. 'ee could not catch the breath any more. Eet got desperate. Now 'ee is …" and the boy looked at the crumpled papers and found a word. "'ee is on the ventilator. They breathe for 'eem."

There was a pause.

"You understand?"

Benji slowly shook his head affirmatively.

"I do not know what to do. Ma mère, she writes. She writes to shed the tears. And, aussi, she must share the tears with me. She cannot see 'eem. No one can see 'eem. There is too much of the daanger. All those near 'eem wear special suit. He is not awake.They make 'eem sleep so they can breathe for 'eem. The machine must do the job."

Another pause.

"Comprenez vous?"

"Benji slowly nodded."

The boy looked down and haltingly spoke to the papers, "Mon père, je t'aime. J'ai peur."

The next few minutes passed without a word. The boy held his hands before him and closed his eyes. He crossed himself. Then Benji moved – moved and spoke.

He looked up to the top of the tree – then at the boy. Benji pointed at the tree. He sat just pointing, then spoke. "It is sacred … protective … for centuries." Benji stared at the top of the tree. "One tree grows a thousand years. It chooses and protects. But here … so rare. How did you find it? How did you know to pray here?"

"I do not know. I walked with the paaper. Suddenly I felt the weakness and I 'ad to seet. I was overcome."

sacred
thoughts

"Ah, the tree found you. She will help you – you and your father."

"The tree found me?"

"Yes, the tree knows. It has ancient knowledge. It has power. It is Pehuén. It is sacred."

"A saacred tree." The boy stared at Benji. "You know thees?"

"Yes. The tree understands. It will help."

"Mon dieu! Merci, mon ami. Merci beaucoup."

Then the boy left.

THIRTEEN   The Favored & Savored Cheek

"Benji, I'm so glad you waited for me. Have you been talking to the trees?"

"I learned some French."

"Oh, which trees speak French?"

"The boy spoke French. The tree speaks Mapudungun … and many other languages. Ancient. It's very rare here. It belongs in Patagonia. It is sacred."

The Araucaria? The Parasol tree?"

"Yes, he prayed under it. His father is in the hospital. He chose the right tree. Or, the tree chose him."

"You were there, you were there with him?"

"Yes, he prayed to his God. I prayed to the tree."

"Oh, Benji. You are so full of surprises!"

"They don't belong here. The trees."

"There's a Norfolk Pine a few miles from here. It is even more particular as to where it grows. You know that the Norfolk pine isn't a pine …"

"Yes, Araucaria." Benji stared back toward the site of the Parasol tree. "I like your name for the tree, the Parasol, much better than, well, the other name doesn't sound sacred."

"Well, the shape, the shape of the really mature ones, only the mature ones. That's what some of the folks in Patagonia called them. When I was there with my father, I remember seeing these trees and disbelieving that they existed. They are so beautiful, so different, so stately. They really looked liked giant parasols. They're threatened, worse, I believe they are endangered, but, even before that, they were protected, protected because of their being sacred to the natives. The natives insisted on their being protected."

"They do the protecting."

"Yes, Benji, the trees can do the protecting, but … only, if we give them a chance."

"I held the boy's shoulder. But I wasn't too close."

"Oh, Benji."

"I don't touch a lot … not people."

"I understand."

"i was afraid he might touch me, my face."

"Your face Benji. What do you mean?"

"It's hard to say."

"That's all right, Benji. You don't have to say anymore if you don't want to."

"I want to, and I don't want to. I want to more. I don't know how."

There was a long pause where they each just kept looking at each other, smiling, looking away, then looking back.

"Let's go take a walk and talk to the trees."

"Good idea, Acacia. We can visit the ancient Ginkgo."

"Talk about going back in time. Okay, Benji, we'll go back before the dinosaurs and visit the Ginkgo."

They strolled from tree to tree, putting their ears to a few, hugging a special one or two, and even conversing with one on their walk. Benji stopped to thank the Parasol tree for helping the boy.

Then they came to the Ginkgo.

"Look at the leaves, Benji. they're like fans. It's so lovely. It looks like a fern."

"Maidenhair."

"Yes, Benji, Maidenhair."

"It's older than the Araucaria."

"Yes, I guess, possibly even before the Mesozoic. You're full of interesting insertions."

"It's a boy, it's OK."

"What do you mean?"

"The girl, when she becomes a woman, when she makes fruit, the smell is … it's not good."

"Oh, yes, now I know. the rotting female fruit can drive people away. It's worse than an unkempt dog kennel. It's a horrible stench."

"That's what I said."

"Yes, Benji, that's exactly what you said. People need to listen to you carefully. You say a lot in a few words."

"Thank you, Acacia."

Acacia lifted her hand to place it on Benji's cheek, but he pulled away."

"I'm so sorry, Benji. I did something wrong."

"No. I don't want to change the cheek, the cheek where you kissed me."

"Oh Benji, I'll fix that."

Then, Acacia planted a series of kisses on each cheek and added one on each ear.

"Now I can't wash my face for a long time."

FOURTEEN   A Need to Play

"They should be here shortly!"

"Who mom? Acacia?"

"No, Benji, I'm sorry. It's Kim and Hyo-joo. They should be here any minute.."

"OK Mom. I'll call Barbara. I can go study."

"Thank you, Benji."

"That's the door. I'll get it Mom."

"Well, I did say shortly."

"Hi Kim, where's Hyo-joo?"

"Hi Benji. she's coming. She wanted to do a little more work on her preparation. There's not much time before the debate or discussion or whatever they are now calling it."

"Disentanglement."

"Benji. you are too much. One word and you give the answer. I should take you back to Korea with me."

"Korea is old like some trees, and older."

"Korea is beautiful, Benji. You should see the pink trees!"

"They are on Nami."

"Nothing escapes you, Benji. Your mind is like a sponge. Ill just toss my coat over here.. Oh no. I forgot. I should put it on the rack. Is your Mom in?"

"Yes, in her room, the kitchen. She likes that. It smells good."

"Yes, of course. And Barbara?"

"She's changing colors on her face."

"I understand. I think I understand. Hyo-joo said you really helped Pierre."

"I don't know Pierre."

"He's the young boy you sat with, the one from France."

"I didn't help. I just listened. Then I told him about the tree. He chose the right tree … or … the tree chose him."

"Ah, yes, the monkey puzzle, a most unusual tree."

"Yes, but Acacia has a prettier name. They call it monkey puzzle because monkeys have trouble; they can't find the hidden food in it. Acacia calls it the Parasol tree. I like that name better. It's pretty, like she is."

"I think if Acacia called it a pine tree, you'd like it better."

"Some people call it Chile Pine. It's sacred."

"You see, Benji, you teach me. I was trying to make a little joke, and you correct me."

" I like jokes."

"Maybe you and I should get together and work on your sister. She could use a few jokes … a little lightening up."

"Oh, Barbara,, there you are. Benji and I were just talking."

"Yes, I heard you. I need lightening up."

Benji caught a nod from Barbara and also caught its intention. "I'm going upstairs. I need to study."

Barabara waved, "Bye, Benji."

"Hyo-joo is coming a bit later. She's still refining her paper for the discussion. She has her bike with the super light, but she might make it here before dark."

"Well, going back will be safer."

"Should I say hello to your mother?'

"Just yell. She's in the kitchen."

"Hello, Mrs. Sappiance. It's Kim. Thank you for having us."

Muffled through the door he heard, "You and Barbara have a nice visit. I'll be with you later."

"She love's her kitchen, Kim."

"Women do."

"No, Kim. Mom loves her kitchen because it's her refuge since our father died. It's the one place where she feels she doing things for him even though he's not here. Half of our meals are *his* old favorites. When you're not here, *his* seat is empty."

"I'm sorry."

"No, need. She will deny anything I've said. I'm just a daughter talking about her kitchen. Now tell me, what do you hear from home?

"Well, you already know about Samchon and his story about the religious woman and all the trouble she spread. So far, Samchon has no illness trouble himself, or none that he writes about. It's always someone else with him. I admire him. I would like to please him, but that would be impossible. I would have to forget about any life abroad, like here and now, and, instead, devote my life to schooling, medicine in Korea … or something else, something hard and demanding."

"It can't be that bad., Kim."

"You're right. He really is fair. I say that because I'm not sure that I want to devote my life to something so strongly. Not yet. He's not just medicine. Now he's all medicine – because of this virus. Other times, he relaxes – a little. He teaches about the arts, paintings, history, pottery, and on and on. He explains how Japan really became civilized and highly cultured because of the influence from Korea. Then Japan tried to invade Korea and failed. Korea was too strong. That was Monkey Face; he was a famous Japanese ruler with a famous and ugly face. Samchon cannot resist teaching and telling stories. It is his life. He loves his country. He loves the people. He says that the very word of his profession explains this. He is a doctor and doctor means teacher. It is a game to him that he cannot stop playing. Please, I understand. He is good. He teaches the right things. But, after awhile, there is too much seriousness; you want another game with more fun."

"You want fun, but you enjoy your Samchon. You do love him."

"Very much."

'You want to be like him."

"No one can be like him."

"You want to serve his cause."

"For sure. But in the next room, not in his footsteps."

"You have to be your own person, Kim."

"That is why I am here."

"In the States."

"No, here, now, that's why I am here with you."

"Oh, Kim, this is getting deep."

"Not really. I see bottom. I see you. I know that you and your culture … well, I know that you are different. You are young but you are an older young. You are wise and serious, but you enjoy playing. You want to go back and be young."

"Please, Kim, you give me too much credit and you read far too much into my desires and intentions. Yes, because of Benji, because we were homeschooled; I say homeschooled, it was a time of readjustment with a pretense at schooling. Because our lives have been different, because out mother needed us more than the school did when father died, or because of whatever, I am older and probably a little too serious for you."

"No, you like the playfulness in me. I can see that."

"I think you like it more than I do. You are brimming with foolishness."

"Ah, yes, but in such an appealing way."

"Yes, Kim, in a very appealing way. But you are older too. Perhaps too old to hunger for play? Aren't you to be 20 this year?"

"No. but Hyo-joo will be."

"Exactly what I mean."

"You see?"

"I see too much. I see that you are too revealing and too appealing. We need to talk about something else."

"Well, let's see, you are as smart as my sister, and everyone says she is smarter than I am. You are prettier than any other girl I know, but that doesn't matter. Being pretty doesn't matter to you." He then looked at her and smirked before going on. "You accept me and my culture. No, you don't accept my culture. You don't like it when I criticize your officials or your policies. You especially don't like it when I criticize your president. Benji likes that but you don't. You are independent. You enjoy a debate; sorry, a discussion about our cultures, just as you do about our futures. You brag about my culture, you point out to others how Korea was the foundation for the arts in Japan, you see how we, in Korea were ahead of China long ago, and you recognize that I want to be part of your culture just as you would like to absorb more of mine. So it seems like we should get to know each other much better. Now, of these subjects, which one would you prefer to follow?"

"Is there a reason that Hyo-joo is coming late?"

"You look too far ahead."

"You leave a trail that is too easy to follow."

FIFTEEN   Surrogate Mother

"I don't know what I'm going to do with you children."

"Ma, we are not children. I make half the meals, I do most of the food shopping, I help clean the house. and I look after Benji."

"Oh, yes, Barbara, I'm sorry. I know. And next year you'll be gone. Well not gone, still here, but in college unless …"

"Oh, Mom, forget the unlesses. The virus is the virus and we'll live with it. Benji spent an afternoon with the math professor at college yesterday and he blew him away."

"Yes, but Benji has his needs."

"Don't make him out to be a baby, Mom. He dresses himself. He washes his own clothes. He may not look like a movie star when he puts it all together, but, hey, it's not bad. He makes his own sandwiches."

"Oh, tuna fish from a can."

"With lettuce, and mayonnaise, and pickle."

"You're right I tend to baby him."

"He's grown Ma. He's a man. I know. There are a lot of parts that are playing catch up. but he has more parts that are way ahead than behind."

"I suppose."

"Mom, since Dad died, well, I shouldn't say this, but I'm going to anyway. Since Dad died, well, in the beginning you had all you could do to hang on. We understood, Mom. And then things got better. We went back to school, and then you got the job at Lexington. So we're all OK. But you forget that a lot of time has passed. Benji has grown up. He's a young man. People his age go into the army! You can't baby Benji anymore."

"Babying Benji? I'm afraid that I left this world the same day your father did. You, well, especially those first years, you had to suddenly grow up, didn't you? I took away your youth. You weren't allowed to have an adolescence. I'm so sorry, Barbara."

"Oh, Mom, I love you so much. You've come back a long way. You almost *did* join dad. Now you're back with us.

"Oh dear, I'm afraid you're right."

"He's got a girlfriend, Ma. Benji has a girlfriend!"

"Acacia? They're friends. They have a lot in common."

"He's taken with her, Mom."

"Oh, dear, I need to open my eyes again. I am still living back with your father – even when I think I've recovered. I miss him so much."

"We all do, Ma, but time moves on."

"And what about you, Barbara. What about you and Kim. Is that serious?"

"I really don't know. I think we each have very serious feelings. We're both young. Kim has to find himself. He's hunting; he's trying. When he does, well, whether I can be with him then, I don't know. I have very strong feelings for him, but I'm afraid of those feelings. If I let them loose, I'm afraid that I'll lose sight of everything else. I'm trying very hard to keep myself under control."

"Oh, I'm so sorry, I've asked you to grow up without giving you a chance to be a foolish girl."

"I don't need to be a foolish girl."

"Hmmm, you know, Barbara, if I hadn't been a foolish girl, I probably wouldn't have married your dad."

"Deep waters. Time for me to do my homework."

SIXTEEN   The Eve

They were on the eve of the debate – or whatever this was to be. It was Friday night, March 13th, a day that would be remembered by many of those at Lexington Prep. One last night of preparation, one last effort to pick out that which would make an impact, and one further chance to anticipate what others might say causing an unexpected reaction from the stage. All this permeated the preparation of the chosen few. The latter consideration was the most troubling. If one person's remarks derailed the rest and put them on a foreign path, what then? They had to be ready for a deflection of their original intentions – and possibly a re-arrangement or even a reversal of what and how something might be said. But this was good. This caused them to listen to others, to read the news, to urge other students to reveal their concerns. Would there be major diversions of the theme? Would there be a crushing of all else due to the litany and prevalence of misleading and false rumors? Could it become overwrought with emotion considering the plight of some families in the harder hit countries?

Now, they were to receive last minute instructions from the faculty advisors. They sat, somewhat apart, using arms for distancing, touching hands, or almost being able to do so, indicated the proper distance. They wanted to set an example. They needed to set an example. They carried disinfectant wipes to use, advocating further prevention. They were told to stress prevention, and everyone of them would adhere to that admonition. They had also been schooled to be thoughtful and compassionate. People were suffering. This was not a place for participants to individually shine but an opportunity to collectively help the whole of the student body, realizing the spectrum it contained. Those had been the preliminary instructions. Now they would receive last minute instructions.

The advisors entered, wearing masks, and seated themselves after widely spacing the chairs. Georges Bonlinguet, a biology teacher with two Master's degrees, and himself from France, rose to speak.

He had lost his accent, yet, his French revealed itself in a delightful, throaty way, complementing a baritone presentation.

"I shall not take long. First a few updates. Our freshman, Pierre, whom many of you know, and, indeed some of you have dearly befriended, had good news from home. His father is off the ventilator and is improving."

There was a meaningful yet subdued applause and an exchange of eye smiles riding over masks.

"I am not aware of any other student with family in such dire circumstance. Do any of you know differently?"

No one responded.

"Hyo-joo, what about you and your family in South Korea. This tsunami of cases from that religious gathering. Did your family escape?"

"Yes sir. My family is well, thank you. The authorities say they have contained the problem … again. It took only one person to start the fire and many to put it out."

"Good. I am pleased for you and your family. Let's all try to be positive tomorrow. Let's show we care. We want to stress education, information, and understanding – understanding of the fear that many have. Let's be compassionate. This is not to be a political debate. This is not a time for demeaning or blaming. Some of our students come from countries where governmental authorities deny the truth. We want to help them but not invite them to get into political trouble. We want our students to understand how to protect themselves and their loved ones, but not risk trouble by confrontation. Is this understood?"

Heads nodded.

"You will each have a wireless microphone. I suggest you wipe it with sanitizer in front of the student body, illustrating a measure of prevention. The microphones should facilitate your speaking through a mask. The weather forecast is favorable. Cool, but favorable. In order to stress the importance of prevention and distancing, the presentation will be outside. We will have monitors checking for distancing."

"Oh, and Larry, I have published your information regarding hand washing, hand hygiene, facial hygiene, and fomites. That was well done. Certainly, you proceed with your talk as planned. We are simply reinforcing your 'Practical Points for Prevention and Protection.' We're sending this to all students in an email."

"That will be sent with our ongoing summary of the current situation from the faculty and school standpoint."

He looked over the group. "Questions? Does anyone have a question or comment? Well, if not, I'll turn this over to Ms. Holcombe for an update of the latest news."

"Thank you. Can you hear me through the mask, speaking into the mike? Way back in the last row, can you hear me clearly?"

"Yes."

"Good. First the States. We previously told you that the US has over a thousand known cases of COVID-19; now it's 1800 and climbing. Today, on Friday the 13th, I hope you aren't superstitious, President Trump declared the COVID problem to be a national emergency. That gives him further authority to act and disperse money to help."

"For those of you that are not clear on the situation, President Trump made an announcement only two days ago that all travel to and from Europe, except for the UK, will be suspended for thirty days starting tonight. That's midnight tonight on Friday the 13th. There are some exceptions to this, largely applying to US citizens. We continually revise the latest information. It's in bold print on our website. So now those of you who are hoping to go back to Europe fall into the same category with the students from China, Iran, and South Korea. We are here to listen and help. We have someone on call to respond to your needs 24 hours a day. We shall work together."

"President Trump continues to go without a mask. This is not to be taken as a guideline."

She paused, scanned the masked faces, and queried, "Any questions regarding the situation in the States?"

A hand rose. The student stood. "Are we going to finish the semester? We hear rumors about all the schools being forced to close."

"We don't know. We are playing this day by day. Each state will be different. It's possible that there will be a mandate. As you know, our neighbor, Massachusetts has been hit hard. She is likely to set a pattern. I expect that most of New England and most of the schools will act in concert. We'll certainly keep you all posted and try to help every way we can. Your safety is our prime concern."

"All right. Let's go abroad. As of two days ago, we officially have a pandemic and WHO has named Europe as the active center of the pandemic. The cases in Europe mow exceed those reported in China. Obviously, all our European students are concerned, if not frightened, and appropriately so. Be especially careful with your colleagues from Spain, Italy, France, and the UK. They are particularly likely to have loved ones at risk."

"And a major point. This is not a disease where young folks, like you, are, immune or with little risk. The virus is acting differently in different countries, but it has been striking people of all ages. Sutton," she addressed a young, dark skinned girl with wide eyes, "I believe that you will take this a step further. This needs to be stressed. Naturally, people with medical problems and the older population are especially vulnerable, and you youngsters can not only catch this virus, but even if you don't get very sick, you can spread it to someone else where it can be devastating. Keep that in mind whether you're here or going back home."

"The virus is spreading everywhere." It's in Africa, Malaysia, Iran (and quite bad there), Brazil, Ukraine, Puerto Rico, and scattered over Eastern Asia. We are trying to keep an up to date log regarding each country for all our concerned students. This means regulations, travel restrictions, or anything that might be pertinent."

"OK. Let's try to keep it positive, mutually supportive, factual, and non-political. Did I give you guidelines? Did I say non-political? Did I say supportive?"

SEVENTEEN   Disentanglement

Barbara and Benji came to the debate. There was only a murmur of a breeze running through the magnificent grounds. The trees stood proudly, hosting this momentous presentation.

"Handouts" were done electronically. They included basic material on viruses, a bit more about coronaviruses, an indication of symptoms that were of concern, and a great deal on prevention – especially on hand hygiene and facial hygiene, but those handouts also drew further parallels with past instructions about travelers' diarrhea and the advisability of keeping other sensible measures in mind. It was a compact, pocket companion snuggly set on the devises which had become part of the anatomy of the student body. This was a viral catechism, and with no shortage of contacts for help.

The audience was all masks and all ears. Benji readjusted his seat so that he might comply with regulations while getting a better view of Acacia. Barbara was a safe six feet from Kim. Kim was filling that six foot gap with chatter that kept Barbara shaking her head – in seeming disbelief.

A boy about the size of Benji held up his hand and waved to him. It was Pierre. Benji replied by holding his hand over his heart.

Mr. Bonlinguet stood. The audience murmur ceased, and only that from the faint zephyr in the trees remained. He introduced each of the presenting students. Then he gave a short explanation of the uncertainty of the times, including even the immediate future for the school. He explained that there were a few alternatives in the offing including continuing where they were with a shortened and somewhat intensive course load in order to insure completion, changing to media teaching, as some schools had done (facilitating continuing the semester irrespective of physical locale), and searching for local housing if the dormitories had to be closed down. He suggested that everyone keep in touch. All the latest updates would be on the school website.

Hyo-joo was the lead off speaker.

"I am here from South Korea, where we have just had a horrible explosion of this virus, all due to the unfortunate action of only one person. Whatever each and every one of us does counts. So I ask you to be knowledgable and be responsible. And yes, also be caring. But be smart in your caring. Hugging an old grandparent may not be good, especially if you have somehow picked up the virus. You don't have to be sick to have the virus. You can have the virus for weeks and never feel sick. So be smart Smart caring is throwing a kiss from twenty feet away."

"Now I shall tell you a secret. It is the secret club of the Coronavirus family. It is called the 5H Club." Then Hyo-joo went through her explanation the 5 H's and the basics of the virus finding a home and starting to replicate. She added how much this virus loved to change and that each time it went through a passage it tended to change. That allowed her to explain, as Kim had suggested, that we have many mutants. She ended with, "You see, we now have at least 10 different strains of the virus that have been recognized; the Chinese one is different from the European one, and we go on and on. Each strain, each mutant, has its own personality and acts differently. When you put that together with each person that it attacks being different, you understand why we have so many different presentations of the virus, and why it is so challenging to understand."

Next, a young man from Puerto Rico spoke. He clarified that he, like Hyo-joo, was a senior, and hoped to graduate. He knew the virus, rather than the school officials, might determine how and whether this happens. He pleaded for patience and mutual support.

Then he went into his talk which was a basic explanation of what a virus is. He pointed out how viruses have only recently been identified and we have both ignorance and knowledge as a result. To explain this, he gave a comparison of the early days of identifying and understanding bacteria. "You see, even the authorities were wrong then. Some of the best educated said that the plague that was killing off large segments of London was from bad air, from "miasma." One man defied them. He is now considered to be the father and founder of public health, but then … then, he was considered to be a maverick, he was denounced as a fool, and his ideas were discounted as trash. This is where I learned the word ca-lum-ni-a-tion;" he struggled, separating the syllables and then repeated the word more smoothly, "it really fits for what they did to this man. He was right; he was alone, but he was right. Where are the voices like his now?"

He ended by pointing out that antibiotics work on bacteria but viruses are different. We don't have good treatments for viruses. While we keep hunting for those good treatments, prevention is the key."

A tall, gangly boy, not quite used to his rapidly extenuating form, took a few spider-like steps to be in better view of the audience. He turned toward the faculty representatives, bowed, and thanked them for the privilege of being in this school. He turned back and thanked the audience for the opportunity to speak to them.

"I am from a very poor country, and only because of much help that comes from here, I can learn with you. My country suffers. She suffers from the virus but I think she suffers more from bad information. People in my country lie. It is not my mother or my sister who lies. It is the big people who lie. If you repeat what they say, you lie. You learn not to listen."

There was a pause. He adjusted his awkward frame. "Even here, we hold in our hands … these." He held up his smart phone for all to see. Standing there, microphone in one hand and smart phone in the other, he faced the smart phone and talked to it. "A gift to me. Wonderful." Then he turned and talked to the audience. "But careful! This is filled with false, bad, and wrong information meant to lead you into dark woods. Our social connections are not where to get health news or medical news. Be careful. Facebook, Twitter, Snapchat, Instagram, and … each and every person you text daily … this is not the place to learn about plague. Things that go viral on the net … they are not the smart news about the virus. People think they know the truth when they don't, and governments, when they know the truth, do not always share it. They have been doing this for centuries."

He ended with, "Over 200 years ago this was written, and I do not quote, but, offer what I think you call a gist, saying something like this." He looked at his notes, and, reading, he continued. "The mischief in contagious disease lies more with alarm and rumor, more with denying its presence, more with blaming others, and doing this rather than trying to find the truth." He paused, and spanned his gaze over the audience. "That was 200 years ago! It was yesterday too."

The next student was from Brazil. She indicated that her government didn't recognize science as we do here. She asked that the students who would be returning to countries like hers be smart in another way. "Don't fight the police, don't fight the army, don't fight the government, fight the virus. First thing is to know what to do and how to do it without inviting someone else to take everything away from you. Your knowledge is your purse. Use it wisely."

Then she went into her core of material, which was a history of epidemics and pandemics. She apologized and said that she would try to take some stories from three books and condense them into ten minutes. She was through in nine. She alluded to the Great Flu of 1918, with a death toll of at least tens of millions – some say 200 million! She mentioned measles, one of the most contagious of all diseases, spread by world explorers. She referred to smallpox which had spread across the world, even in blankets – infected blankets given to natives. Then she spoke of the iron lungs, our four term president, and polio … polio leaving a paralyzing path. She chose these nasty scourges not because they had left such a mark, but because they had taught us how to fight and survive. We can do it again. She ended with, "And so you see, now we have vaccines for flu, measles, and polio, and we don't need one anymore for smallpox. We do have hope."

"I love those positive remarks, don't you?" The girl bounced to the front and addressed the group. "My name is Sutton. I am here at Lexington now for two years, and I have two more years to go." Her eyes were large, black, and dominating. Her voice ended each sentence with an elevation, like a swing. "My family moves very frequently, but, here, I stay in one place with you. We are family here. My mother travels with doctors to needy places, sometimes very dangerous places, dangerous because of contagion, but also dangerous because of people not understanding when others are trying to help. They become frightened. When we don't understand things, we are scared. If we are trying to explain things, complicated things, like this disease, we need to listen as well as talk. My mother taught me this when I traveled with her. It was easier then because the disease was easier to understand. This one has so many faces!"

"They say children don't get it. They do. Children do get it and they have strange ways of showing they are sick. My mother is seeing children who have high fevers, strawberry tongues, and red palms and soles. It looks like something she knows, but this is different. She says it is the new great imitator! It is the virus looking like, and pretending to be, another. My mother is a doctor, but she is learning. This is new. The virus is teaching her. Other children have it a different way. Some have their hands and fingers swell up and turn red. This looks like another disease we know but it is different. What is important is that we are all learning, every day we are learning. We try to teach others when we don't have the whole story. We have to admit that. We don't have many answers. This is not like measles or smallpox where it is easy to tell if you have it. This is confusing. If we don't pretend to have answers when we really don't, and if we listen to others to hear their fears, we may sound like we aren't smart, but this is being smart."

"If we are patient and listen, we learn. If we listen and care, we help."

Then it was Acacia's turn. Her voice boomed out of that small body, joining her enthusiastic embellishment with her arms. "The people you meet here, the friends you make, the bonds that you tie, they will stay with you the rest of your life. These are very troubled times and we will all return to different places – very different places, and some very troubled places. Some of you will be in the caldron with the virus. Our hearts go with you. Take us with you, keep us with you, and keep in touch. We can continue to help. We do continue to care."

Then, Acacia gave an explanation of the Coronavirus family, the four Greek divisions, the many animal species afflicted by the virus, and the value of listening to people with special knowledge, like veterinarians and historians. She reviewed the anatomy of the coronavirus briefly, indicating that it had a lipid capsule, a capsule that was broken down by washing with soap and water. "You see, anatomy is important, even when you can't see what you are describing."

She gave examples of epidemics in piglets and cattle, and she pointed out how the virus can have a reservoir in the gut and spread through the stool. This naturally led her to emphasize hand washing, fomites, and mask use. "It's all common sense when you learn the basics and ignore the rumors," she emphasized.

She referred to reinfection in cattle, indicating that we cannot be complacent. "This is not like some infections where once you have it, you've had it, and then, you're over it. We are constantly learning about this one."

"We have tried different vaccines in our domesticated animals. We learn from them, our friends."

She stressed how sheep and cows have feelings just as we do. She recalled a ewe who had lost her young – filling the pasture with her plaintive cries for a full day. "You'd be surprised at how many critters, plants, and pets are really like us. You just have to look and listen. We learn from them. Just as we learn about the disease from them … we learn about caring."

"Listen to those who hurt. Show them you care. That will help them to get through the troubled times. That will help them to heal. Your listening, your understanding, your friendship, your love, those are the best pills. Stay in touch with each other and show that you care."

Benji held his head down and found tears rolling over his mask.

Larry got up and presented his many steps for prevention. He had a broad enigmatic grin that previewed how he would deliver his message. He stressed hand washing and how to do it, singing a ditty, well off key, which was just under a half minute long; that was the needed time to scrub. Not only was the ditty poorly sung, but interrupted by his puffing and blowing on a bubble pipe to indicate the need for lots of suds! He then added the use of wipes as a back up for those times where washing was impossible – juggling three (presumably weighted examples) to emphasize their crucial role. He discussed different cautions for private and common bathrooms, keeping toothbrushes from being fomites from aerosolized and infected stool. Here, to make his point he tried brushing while using an encased brush – evoking another anticipated chuckle from the audience. To underscore safe distancing, he pulled a tape between his outstretched hands and then read it. "Yes, indeedy, the distance needed." He suggested sniff and swallow as opposed to blowing of noses, disposable tissues rather than washable hankies, keeping your hands from your face, pretending you're like a dog with one of those clear plastic hoods over your head, and then sure enough, he had one as a prop. He stressed avoidance and care of fomites stressing handrails and doors saying he always picked a big fellow to be in front of him as he descended stairs, a nice cushion to fall into. He apologized, noting that it was their age group that was most likely to be lax and most needed to be exemplary – especially when encountering vulnerable and aged relatives … adding, "It's only the mean relatives where you break the rules."

The student body loved it but Benji was still listening to Acacia, repeating in his mind, each word, still alive, still vibrant.

EIGHTEEN   Dominoes

It was only a weekend, but, on that following Monday, a series of dominoes started to fall; the virus had pushed the first one, and that was enough.

On that Monday, March 16th, 2020, Maine *recommended* closing of its schools. On that same Monday, New Hampshire *ordered* closure of its schools. On the next day, Tuesday, the 17th, Connecticut and Massachusetts *ordered* the closure of their schools. Nearby New York followed the next day. Here in southern Rhode Island, it was a time of turmoil and expectation. Hectic plans were being made only to be altered. No plan seemed secure. As it turned out, there was only a week from the falling of the first domino to the feared and awaited nudge on the last, lone Lexington piece. Much like the contagion had spread the virus, this sudden and severe reaction to its devastation disseminated, powered by its own momentum. That last domino did not stand proud but stood shaken and wavering, just waiting for a nudge.

NINETEEN   Widowmaker

"Benji will be so disappointed that he wasn't here to receive you, Acacia. He's cleaning out his locker at the high school. As you know, he's not the most talkative person, but after your presentation on Saturday, well, he just went on and on. We all enjoyed it. And the whole presentation was just beautifully executed. But. as far as Benji was concerned. I think his ears opened up only once."

"Oh, I'm sorry to hear that, Mrs. Sappiance. I thought all the presentations were wonderful. Many students felt so supported, and, it was critical to give them support, to show understanding. I particularly enjoyed Maria's presentation. She was the girl from Brazil, you remember. I thought that she reached out and found all those who were going to hostile environments. She is very wise and she is only 17."

"Of course, Acacia, you are right. I was, well, if I compliment myself, I would say I was using a bit of hyperbole for effect. If I were a bit more ingenuous, I'd probably say, I love my son too much."

There was a long pause. Mrs Sappiance busied herself with a recipe book and a few spices that she picked from the cupboard. Acacia stared into space and finally faced her teacher.

"I am the one at fault."

"What happens to you now, Acacia. Where do you go?"

"My road is easy, Mrs Sappiance. Unlike so many, I have many wonderful choices. My father wants me to join him in doing his research in the forests. I would be his gofer. But, while doing all the "scut" work, I would be learning. And I would be working in a beautiful environment. This wouldn't be the first time. I've done this before. I've done it many times, perhaps too many. But … while I dearly love my father, I do need a break, and I do need a place to find myself. That's where Lexington has been a big help. I see myself not as a little cripple. Sorry, I don't want to sound maudlin. My father has been very protective. Perhaps too protective. I don't know whether he feels guilty that I have problems, he feels needed because my mother is gone, or … he's just lonely. But none of those things address my needs directly. I need to be able to launch out on my own. My uncle, he's another lonely one, but he's also another one filled with offerings and devoted … he and my father are married to their fields. He loves his cows, his pigs, his horses, and whatever animals he is working with at the time. I am one of the few people that he really gets along with; I can see that. Well, you see, Mrs. Sappiance, I have no shortage of opportunities and these are safe and well away from other people, replacing them with cows sheep, or trees."

"When did you lose your mother?"

"I was twelve. She was working, helping my father. A 'widow maker' fell on her."

"I'm so sorry, dear."

"One fell on my legs when I was four."

"Oh, dear!"

"I used to love trees and then I seemed to hate trees. Then I didn't know how I felt. Benji really changed that. He helped me. I realized it wasn't the tree's fault. Benji gave me a new lens. I can turn it each way. I can get close to the tree and feel it like Benji does, I can turn it the other way and see the big family; and then I can see it as it affects me. I can see it looking at the the tree, the tree's family, and then back again at me. I was searching for a place … and something … to study. That's when I turned to viruses. I thought they would be less threatening and easier to study. How ironic! Benji brought me back to my earlier love. I realize now that my searching was more for myself."

"And what *do* you think you will do now, Acacia?"

"I don't know. I even think that just being out in a forest all by myself, living with the trees, making friends again … there are some openings our West. As long as they don't see my picture, my height. I'm really very self sufficient. I just move a little slower."

"You don't think you'd be lonely?"

"When Benji gets lonely, or feels threatened, he retreats into himself. I understand that, Mrs Sappiance. I do that too. He does cubes I do other things. We just try to find ourselves."

"You don't think leaving your friend, Benji, will be difficult?'

"That's why I have come here. I need to talk to him. I need to feel what he wants for me and for himself."

"Oh my, Barbara was right."

"What do you mean?"

"Barbara sees me as having been frozen when my husband – their father – died. She became a mother. She never had the childhood, or, really, adolescence she deserved."

widowmaker

"Oh, Barbara still has a child in her that she brings out. You need to watch her with Kim."

"That's another problem, isn't it?"

"Barbara will manage and Kim will manage. They are both very resilient."

"I really enjoy talking with you, Acacia. Can you stay for supper?"

"May I look at that recipe book?"

TWENTY   The Return of Tommy

"What are ya carryin' there stupid?"

Benji looked only half way toward the voice. He knew who spoke. No mask could hide that voice and that voice was muffled by no mask. The lack of mask was as predictable as was the unforgiving nature of the encounter.

"Hey, you stupid shrimp, I'm talkin' to you."

Benji held his books, notebooks, and other accessories very tenuously. He turned his head away from Tommy. He kept walking, but maneuvered the rear of his head toward Tommy. Face to the left, body moving ahead, he crabbed away from threat.

"Well, little wimp, I'm lookin' aroun' and I don't see that dike of a sister. Looks like yer on yer own. Ya know what that means. We're goin' to pick up where we left off."

Benji kept inching forward, with short, stuttering steps, books and paraphernalia piled in his arms, and face kept to port side.

Suddenly, he felt a piercing pain in his right leg and fell.

"How do ya like that shrimp? I learnt that heel kick watching' yer dike sister."

Books and accoutrements lay strewn before him. Then he felt a stinging thud on the back of his left thigh.

"Hey, I'm gettin' pretty good at this kickin' crap. You'll have to tell yer sister."

Trying to collect his things, Benji reached out only to have his arm kicked. He drew his arms in from his belongings, tightly holding the one book that was left of the lot. He kept his face down and away from Tommy. As he rose to his knees, he expected another blow any second, but, surprisingly, he regained a foothold.

"Turn around little man. Yer about to get a piece of the big Tom. Then I'm goin' to take down yer pants and see if ya got any hair over yer johnson."

Benji turned, very slowly at first, then, gripping the book tightly, he finished the turn suddenly, whipping the spine of the book smack against the nose of his opponent, the same nose his sister had found weeks ago. Tommy fell, and as he did, Benji jumped up in the air and came down with both feet squarely on Tommy's generative organs, losing his balance and falling on top of his adversary as he did this. While reluctant to look directly at his face, Benji pushed himself up and nonetheless noted a generous amount of blood coming from Tommy's nose. There was a long moan, a moan that continued to pervade the scene as

Benji picked up his books and accessories. And then, without looking back, he walked home.

TWENTY ONE   The Johnson Jump

"Benji, you're limping. What happened?"

"Ma, he's not just limping. His books are covered with dirt, his forehead is scratched, and Lord knows what else. Were you hit by a car, Benji? What happened? Your arm is bleeding!"

"Ah ook ar ah em"

"Benji, the mask is all crushed against your face. I can't understand you. Take the mask off." Barbara took charge, She took the dirty books and placed them on the hall bench.

"I took care of him. I broke his nose again and jumped on his johnson."

"You did what.?"

Mother intervened with, "Who's he talking about?"

"Thomas, Mom. Thomas Brandos. He's the bully that picks on people like Benji. You remember when he picked on Benji before. I broke his nose."

"More." Benji added

"Now he picks on Benji in order to get back at me. Tell us what happened, Benji."

"He tried to be like you. He kicked me, he kicked me again, then I fell. Then he kicked me again."

"Oh Lord, we better get you cleaned up dear."

"Hang on, Mom. I think there's more to this and I don't think Benji is so badly off after all."

Acacia came in from the kitchen. "Oh, Benji, what happened?"

"I beat Tommy up. I can protect you."

"Benji!" Barbara demanded. "Exactly what happened? You said you broke his nose again!"

"I hit him with my dictionary. He fell and I jumped on his johnson. I can take care of myself."

Kim, who had been listening from a distance, added, "It sounds like he got the word from you, Benji."

Benji smiled and Barbara admonished Kim, "You're incorrigible."

"My body is growing. It's strong. I didn't cry. I fought."

"Oh, Benji!" Acacia flew and hugged him.

"So much for social distancing," Kim remarked.

TWENTY TWO   Light From the Limbo Window

Kim and Hyo-joo were temporarily housed in an "in law" apartment belonging to Ms. Holcombe at Lexington Prep. It was not used initially for a mother in law but for Ms Holcombe's son and his wife before they had job changes. It was more than adequate for the Korean twins.

Ostensibly, Hyo-joo took charge of investigating their eventual options, managing their day to day needs, and criticizing Kim. Kim took charge of the exercise equipment and visiting Barbara, and he spent the wee hours on the computer. This proved to be providential.

The question of their next step certainly remained in limbo. Arrangements were made to take advantage of this traffic light holding everyone in place. There was no promise of return to South Korea in the immediate future; there was no place else to go; so at Lexington, a course continuation and possible completion was designed, and a media monitoring of their progress was arranged. There was still the possibility of graduating – even if graduating from a closed school.

So, the Korean twins were in limbo. They had no certain home, no certain travel anticipations, and no certainty that this semester at school would come to fruition. Plans were altered daily. The good news from home was that the tremendous surge in COVID cases at the start of March had come under control. That which had presumably been precipitated by an overly religious act was now contained, even though the casualty numbers in its wake were truly disheartening.

Kim, then, found a way to possibly complete his year. He took advantage of Hyo-joo's communications with Samchon, and, when Hyo-joo became engrossed in her work trying to pack in enough to graduate, Kim spent hours questioning and analyzing answers from Samchon. This was a natural opening and a natural path for him. He started chronicling the history of coronaviruses in South Korea. He took Samchon's words and maneuvered them to seem like his own. For those burning questions that remained, he searched the computer through the wee hours. This turned out to be a most fortuitous step.

After briefly chronicling the story he had heard so many times, the threat of SARS 1 that Korea had essentially escaped and the unfortunate impact of MERS, the stories Samchon had imbedded in their minds, he went on to simply tell the story that Samchon had continued to relate. The computer allowed him to embellish this with facts – indeed facts, dates, figures, and comparisons. At first, this was more of a game. He started with the first case in South Korea and duly noted his starting gate: that case in South Korea was the same day as was the first case in the States. That provided a great comparison. At first, he did this to satisfy himself. Then he took his notes to his advisor and, to his surprise , realized that if he were to carry this to fruition, this could be a means of finishing his schooling at Lexington. He could abbreviate other tasks and concentrate on this. Or, it least it seemed that such might be the case. He, being Kim, decided to throw his chips on the "might be" and hope for the best. He put all his late night efforts into the paper. He was writing, rearranging, editing, crumpling, and restarting a paper which he never expected to write. Soon, he found that the paper was directing him rather than the reverse. He had found a cause which grew and took over. He found something larger than himself.

He shared a minimum of this with Barbara at first, fearing his enthusiasm would wane. As his involvement grew, he shared more, and as he did so, the bond between him and Barbara became tighter and more secure. She was taken aback at how responsible he had become in so little time. He didn't see himself as having changed. Still, he was very pleased with her response.

TWENTY THREE   Back to the Woods

"My father wants me to drive home. Well, to drive up to the forest he is presently camping in."

"Then you will leave me?"

"If I were to go, Benji, then, yes, I would go back to the woods and work with him."

"You could take me, Acacia."

"I don't want to go. I don't want to leave you."

"You can stay."

"He says he wants me to help with his research on the trees. He's working on the spruce bud worm. Everything they've done, all the poisons they've introduced, the only result seems to be a killing off of Ospreys and other vulnerable species while they make spruce bud worms stronger. He wants someone to slog through the woods with him, help with the collection of data. Well … that's what he says. I think he's concerned and feels I'd be safer in the woods, away from people and the virus. I'm not sure where he is. Somewhere in northern Maine or maybe even in Canada. He doesn't stay in one place long. Accommodations vary from meager to none. The common denominator is Woodsman's Fly Dope and DEET. I've done this many times with him in the past, so I do know what to expect. I love the woods. And you've helped me to love the trees again. Still, I don't think he really needs me that much. I think he just feels guilty. Down deep, I expect he feels he has to take care of me."

"I can take care of you."

"I know, Benji. I still have to answer him. I have to pretend it's all about the spruce trees and the work he's doing."

"I know spruce trees. In Maine, white, red, and black. Sometimes red and black mate. Black tastes bad. Animals don't eat it unless they are starving. Spruce bud worms eat white spruce and red spruce. Spruce trees use fungi to talk to each other. I know spruce trees. I can help. I can go with you."

"Oh, Benji. What *am* I to do *with* you? And what can I do *without* you?"

"Spruce make terpenes, they're rain makers. Spruce bud worms hide under bark in the winter. They come out in spring. They hurt the trees."

"You probably know more about spruce trees than my father. Don't worry, Benji. I don't want to leave you any more than you want to leave me. I love you, Benji. You know that."

Benji stopped talking. He held his head half down, looking at the space between them. Under the mask, his lips turned into a wide smile.

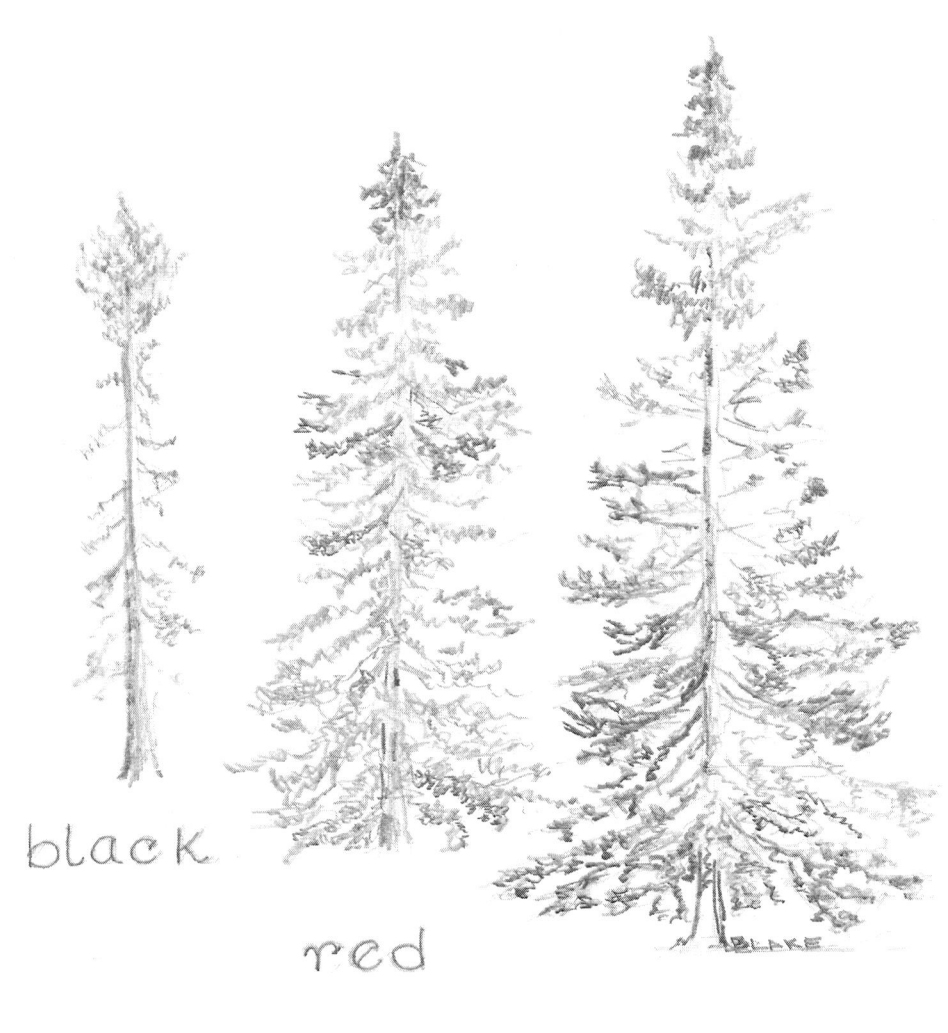

black

red

white

TWENTY FOUR   Bad News & Good News

"I've got bad news and good news, Mom."

"Oh dear. How bad is the bad news?"

"Not a biggie, Mom. It's about Kim. And it's about me."

"Oh, this sounds very big."

"Kim's graduating. So is Hyo-joo."

"That's the good news."

"Yes, Ma, that's some of the good news. Kim wrote a special paper for his final work at the school. It's about the coronaviruses and COVID-19. I think it got him a scholarship, Mom."

"In Korea?"

"No, Ma, here in the States. No one knows when the universities will be opening doors again, or how they will operate, but this is very promising."

"What's the bad news?"

"It's not exactly close by. Hyo-joo is going to a different school – if that one opens in the fall."

"And the bad news?"

"I've applied there as well … to the one where Kim has the scholarship. I've been accepted. I have a scholarship too. Not a big one like Kim. He has a free ride. Still, if I wait tables or do something like that, it won't cost you anything."

"How far away is it?"

"Just a day's drive. Just a day's drive, Mom."

"Oh dear, I'm losing both of you."

"No, Mom. You're not losing anyone."

Kim Finds a Way to Graduate

APPENDIX   Kim's graduation paper

I want to thank my uncle-doctor for all he has done in sharing information about coronaviruses and how they have affected South Korea and her people. He has guided me to investigate with a passion and to write with an ability that I didn't know I possessed. All the words over three syllables, I owe to him, all the medical references came from him, and all the bad English, I owe to him.

A word regarding complicated terminology:

Naming of the coronaviruses has not been consistent, logical, or clear. They are a large family, generally divided into four groups, two have been especially devastating: the alpha to domestic animals, and the beta to man. It is in the beta group that we find SARS, MERS, & COVID-19. SARS stands for Severe Acute Respiratory Syndrome. MERS stands for Middle East Respiratory Syndrome

Alternative names such as SARS-CoV-1, SARS-CoV-2, ARDS, novel coronavirus, MERS-CoV, may occur. In other documents, we find Corona virus, corona virus, novel corona virus. the separation or conjunction of the two words, corona and virus shows no singular pattern, but the words are often joined. The name of the current cause of this pandemic, COVID-19, came only after a series of preliminary names. COVID-19 refers to COrona VIrus Disease-2019.

ACE2 stands for angiotensin converting enzyme 2 and is an attachment that is sought by coronaviruses SARS-1 and COVID-19.

KCDC is Korean Center for Disease Control.

Kim Sang-ook Park

INTRODUCTION

Samchon, my uncle and doctor, has filled me with history and facts. He would be disappointed (and show it in a long face) if I did not share a bit of this with you. I shall borrow some of his big words and his wonderful ideas. I shall pretend I have just listened to Samchon give one of his introductions and try to be his second voice. Viruses in the past have shaped history; Samchon has told me this countless times. I am but a hopefully graduating student from a secondary school system, but a true admirer of science and medicine, and especially of those practitioners, like Samchon, who have dedicated their lives to helping others. He holds my hand and guides my words as I write this.

Were it not for yellow fever and its toll taken by the French forces in Haiti, the Louisiana purchase, would not have been readily offered by Napoleon. This allowed President Jefferson to expand the empire of the United States from the Caribbean to Canada and to the West.

Had it not been for smallpox, another virus, the Aztecs would not have interpreted that this was a religious sign: their native gods had failed. They soon adopted the various Christian saints but modified them to fit with their own as a compromise.

The yellow fever noted above was a two edged sword. African blacks were relatively resistant. That resulted in a demand for them as imported slaves. They were resistant to infection and strong workers, highly sought to escalate economy.

Measles, one of the most infectious of all diseases, was an instrument of conquest far stronger than the blunderbuss or cannon.

And, in spite of the countless soldiers dying in WWI from gas or gun, influenza, the Great Influenza of 1918, took far more lives. The death toll there has been variously touted from 20 to 200 million with most authorities compromising at somewhere between 50 and 100 million. This is where irony joined tragedy – bringing all those young men together in such close quarters.

We could speak of other viruses, but these few serve the purpose of indicating how each has dominated a period of history, changed the path of nations, re-arranged religions, altered economies, devastated cultures and sacrificed races into slavery. So when we look at what is happening to our current problem with SARS-2, we should keep history in mind.

Yet, there is one more consideration. Just as the Aztecs interpreted the plague of smallpox as religious retribution, so society have misinterpreted other viral invasions and acted disproportionately or inappropriately. The militia stopped people from fleeing yellow fever-stricken Memphis in 1878, smallpox infected blankets were "beneficently" distributed to native American tribes, and a blockade was mounted in New York City to prevent people leaving due to polio.

Repeatedly, we have seen militant resistance emerge against vaccination whether it was smallpox, influenza, or another similar scourge. Then, anti-vaxers suffered as the viruses sought *them* out.

Fake cures were touted and dollars collected. Every microbe gathered its soapbox of 'expert' curers as it did daily victims. People who were expert in one field were unfortunately deemed to be knowledgeable in another. Some cures were as bad as the disease itself, and the gold standard of medicine, the one my Samchon drums into our ears, primum noc nocere, Latin for "first do no harm," was forgotten.

The culture of politics, prejudice, and propaganda continued. This is where we need even more immunity. We need a vaccine for the misinfodemic.

So, it is with this introduction, but with this nudge from my uncle for us to remember history.

CORONA AND KOREA: DEVASTATION BY AN INVISIBLE ENEMY

On January 19th here in the States, and on that same day, which was January 20th in South Korea, each country had their first blow from COVID-19. Each initial, index case was 35 years old, each one presented as being ill and seeking medical help. The response from each country was different.

In the States, in Seattle, Washington, it was a man who entered an urgent care clinic complaining of a cough and fever for four days. That same day, a woman arrived at Incheon Airport in Seoul, South Korea with a fever. Each of these individuals had arrived from Wuhan, China. He, the man in Seattle, received a battery of tests for various illnesses which were negative and a test for COVID-19 which was positive. She, the woman in Seoul, was tested for COVID-19 and was positive.

In the States, the President announced, "It's one person coming in from China. We have it under control. It's going to be just fine."

In Korea, the KCDC was unleashed, all contacts were traced, and all those identified were isolated. This was Korea's mantra: **Test, Trace, and Isolate**. They had been burned by MERS. They didn't want it to happen again.

Then, as the virus spread in the States, there was great controversy over the degree of threat. On February 28th, President Trump, in referring to the then named Coronavirus said that this virus is " … going to disappear. One day, it's like a miracle, it will disappear."

At that time, the US had tested a total of some 3,300 people and the tests received a considerable degree of criticism. At that time, South Korea was testing better than 10,000 a day including drive throughs – with reliable tests.

But with all that South Korea did, why and how did they have so much trouble soon thereafter?

There is much irony in this.

It is said that one or more attendees to one ceremony of a singular religious group ignited another blaze. This group, the Shincheonji, Church of Jesus, and a holder of still many other titles, had a longstanding reputation. It has been said by past adherents that the leaders of this group demanded roll call where every-one had to physically swipe in and out of services. The message was, sick or not, you were to come to service, if not on Sunday, you were to come on the following Monday. Attendees sat on the floor, packed like sardines in a can, and remained there for hours as the service continued. They were not allowed to wear masks. This is how it was described by a previous adherent. This was an incubation chamber.

South Korean authorities say that this was the source of a terrible secondary spread. All services and gatherings were subsequently shut down. The shut down involved over a thousand religious facilities. There was a battle between the government and the religious leaders. The police knocked on doors, tracked individuals, checked camera footage, and dealt with highly resistant and faithful adherents. The police and the public health officials had one major objective: identify all who have been ill and identify all their contacts – eventually aiming to have these people self isolate. They followed their mantra: test, trace, and isolate. The adherents shouted rights of privacy and religious freedom. South Korean citizens signed petitions calling for the dissolution of the Shincheonji religious sect. It takes 200,000 signatures to induce governmental action from a petition. They had over 500,000 signatures early on.

So we see here why there was a second wave of this affliction in South Korea. History was repeating itself. As with MERS, where just one person who had traveled from the Saudi peninsula caused an epidemic in South Korea, here again it took only one to cause a major surge. It is noteworthy that the government officials were adamant in their stance and finally successful in quelling the second wave.

Was there any similar problem in the States? There was no religious group that received similar blame, but there were others. There were unfortunate gatherings of large groups, large groups inviting unfortunate connections – large groups exhibiting the same irony as that experienced in South Korea.

In Massachusetts, a neighboring state to our school, a meeting was held by, of all things, a biotechnology firm in late February. Massachusetts had confirmed their first case February first. They had a flare in case numbers in early March. Most of those cases from that flare were traceable to the company meeting of the biotech firm. So, where there was a close gathering seeking religious relief in Korea, there was a similar assemblage of people looking for scientific solutions in Boston: each spreading the disease instead of offering cures.

But the irony does not stop there. People seeking to get away from cities, conferences, massive religious gatherings, and their usual, familiar sites, were promised exotic visits and fresh, salt air, only to find that the cruise ships that they were on proved to be another incubating chamber. While known for their having home affiliation apart from the United States, and escaping regulations accordingly, these ships left ports where the gangplanks filled the ships with countless souls from the United States. It would take only one such soul, either entering, or already onboard, to initiate another impressive wave of disease.

Similarly, the ports of call for the cruise ships were subject to unwitting visitation by infected passengers – leaving a wake of disease dissemination.

In February, the largest cluster of cases outside of mainland China was on The Diamond Princess. This ship carried over three and a half thousand people and, before ending its cruise, approximately 20% of those on board tested positive for the virus. Together with another ship, the Grand Princess, these two sailing ladies accounted for more than 800 COVID-19 cases, and ten deaths by the time we, at Lexington were giving our student presentations on the disease on March 13th.

The conclusion here is that cruise ships are, only too often, a logical and predictable setting for outbreaks of infectious disease due to their having a multitude of travelers from varied lands and then congregating teen closely. As pointed out my public health authorities, this is augmented through buffets, shows, limited ventilation, common restrooms, and commonly handled areas like handrails.

So while Korea had her problems with too many people gathering too closely to pray, the States, and other countries were seeing a similar problem with too many people gathering too closely to sail, and others gathering too closely – so that any protective measure would fail. Too many people being too close spells too much trouble.

The States also had problems with other sites of congestion. Just as Boston had its flare with one major gathering, other cities, and their inherent congestion, made control nearly impossible. Convalescent hospitals and prisons proved to be hotbeds for the virus. Congestion is the tinder that allows the fire of the virus to spread.

Lax regulation, congestion, and inadequate testing defeats the first step of the big three: testing and identification. Without that, the second step of tracing, let alone the third of isolating become impossible.

Coronaviruses are a large family. They have been around since prehistoric times. They have infected many animals other than man, and those strains that have infected man, up until more recent times, have usually caused minor problems like colds.

Still, cows and sheep and other animals have been seriously struck by this family and millions of pigs died in just one year as a result of a Corona virus epidemic.

People have been badly struck too, This is the third time. The first time, South Korea was almost entirely spared. That was SARS1 or Severe Acute Respiratory Syndrome One. That was in 2002 to 3. That started in China. Then there was MERS, or Middle East Respiratory Syndrome. That was from 2012 to15. That is when South Korea learned her lesson. It took only one traveler from Saudi Arabia, to start an epidemic in South Korea. A lesson was learned. Our officials watched China, knowing that China was likely to be the source for another coronavirus coming to South Korea.

That was the background for this first case in January.

My sister and I were in school in the United States when this happened. We saw it from the point of view of the Americans.

We also heard from home. Our uncle is a doctor and an expert, and he kept us informed as to the situation in South Korea. In the beginning, our parents were identified as some of the early contacts and they were voluntarily isolated. This is another word for being quarantined.

We seemed to have control. Then there were further cases, the ones from the religious gatherings. The gatherings were so large, the contacts so many, this was a most difficult tracing for authorities. A thousand or more people at a gathering and thousands of such gatherings. Containment seemed impossible.

At our school in the States we heard about the spread and terrible things the virus was doing. We had fellow students from all over the world; so they had unfortunate stories from home – and home was sometimes France, sometimes Italy, Brazil, Spain, or England. So we had a taste of sorrow from around the globe.

Then, as they had in Korea, schools closed in the States. Travel was frozen. That's when this paper started. The virus had spread and was spreading further. That was in mid March of 2020.

Not being a doctor, I can't explain about the medical part of the virus. But I can copy a few of the words and feelings that my doctor-uncle passed on to me. Trust me, my uncle spared little in detail as he kept us informed. Nonetheless, in order not to go beyond bounds, I shall confine myself to those notes that he stressed. He, our Samchon as we call him back home, dealt with all three of the bad coronaviruses. I shall try to explain the most important of things as he explained them to me. I shall also steal from my sister, Hyo-joo. She makes viruses easier to understand. I'll start with that.

Viruses can't live alone for long. Depending upon where they are, they may last for a few hours or a few days. They sit somewhere hoping they can find a cell to live in. Not any cell will do. They look for special cells. The coronavirus family particularly likes the cells in the respiratory tract and the gut of people – and other animals. They have special connections there. But they have to get there. Once they do get there, they take over a cell and make it do only one thing: make new viruses; hundreds and thousands of new viruses. How does it go from this resting place where it is otherwise likely to die, how does it find the right cell? As my sister, Hyo-joo says, it Hitch Hikes a ride. Someone touches the virus where it was left on a railing and now has it on their hand. Then it finds a Highway. It needs a good, easy path, so the contaminated hand touches the mouth and nose; now the virus has a Highway. But it needs to find a cell it can take over, a Home. It slides down the Highway and ends up in the lung; that's one of its favorite cells. Then it Hijacks that cell into doing nothing but making new viruses. That's my sister Hyo-joo's 5H club for the coronaviruses.

The home that the virus is looking for, as my uncle puts it, has "hook ups to fit with the prongs coming out of the crown of the virus." MERS look for special cells that are a little different; SARS1 and COVID-19 (aka SARS-2) like the same cell attachments. These are called ACE2 receptors by the scientists. They lie in the back of the throat, in the upper and lower respiratory tree, in the stomach, in the lower bowel, in the heart, in the lining of blood vessels, the lining of the eye, around the area where we have smell and taste, in the liver … well, you get the idea. This is the home real estate that my sister is referring to. You give a ride to the virus to get there and bingo, the virus latches on and hijacks those cells, and now you have a virus-making factory.

As my sister, Hyo-joo puts it, once the cell is taken over, there is only one drum beat in the factory: replicate, replicate, replicate; all day and all night, nothing but replicate.

My uncle points out that coronaviruses love to change. When they are going from one sick animal or person to another, they have a great tendency to change. Some people call these mutations, Some call them strains. Some use the word genome. Whatever you call them, they are different. And each different strain tends to act differently. That's why we see so many variations as to how this virus acts. With each change, you have new antigens; so now you have to make new antibodies. With each change, you have new viral preferences for certain tissues and organs, with each change, you see possible changes in its strength, its virulence. So, when the coronavirus changes even more by combining with other viruses, we see the possibility for still more variations.

When it likes the gut, it causes vomiting and diarrhea. When it lands in the lung it causes cough and trouble breathing. The worst forms tend to change the lung so it looks like ground glass and can no longer do its job of trading gases; this is a kind of fast acting stiffening and hardening of the lungs. It can cause so much trouble with breathing that some people have to have a machine to help them breathe. One of our student friends had a father who needed that. Fortunately, he got better. My uncle points out that even the machine may not be enough in some cases. In severe cases, the blood is removed from the body, oxygenated, and then returned. This is where the lungs have completely failed.

The coronavirus also has a special preference to interfere with smell and taste. This is a red flag for the virus. These places where it attacks are much the same in other animals. It causes trouble with coughing, pneumonia, vomiting, and diarrhea in cows, pigs, and sheep too. I don't know if they have trouble with taste or smelling.

The special tendency to go to both the gut and the respiratory parts of the body is unusual, but evidently somewhat predictable since the virus is looking for those special hook ups. If the virus hits the lining of the blood vessels, any place that they serve can be affected, so you see how complicated and varied the attack of this plague can be. That's the coronavirus.

For some reason that is not clear to me or that Samchon has explained but I have not understood, all three of the serious human coronaviruses have a tendency to strike the nervous system. Sometimes they do this early and sometimes they leave lasting effects. Some can even last permanently.

We can also say that some people have the virus and don't feel sick; even so, those people who feel fine and have the virus can spread it. And when it spreads to someone else, that person may get very sick – or die.

Now we can get back to what was happening in March with the virus. Here, I'll go back to the news as we received it.

Active cases in South Korea peaked in mid March and have declined since then in spite of a few flares.

As noted, the churches were a major problem with the resurgence of the virus in March. As March drew to a close, the KCDC implemented new quarantine rules for entrants to the country and imposed a cost of 100,000 won per day for staying quarantined in a government provided facility. Those who violated the COVID regulations faced fine and/or imprisonment.

In March, South Korea passed laws forcing people to cooperate in being tested for the virus, and it banned entry into the country for those suspected of being ill. The government released over one hundred billion won for coronavirus prevention and control and fifty trillion won (US$39 billion) for small and medium company support.

In April, it was discovered that over 100 patients who had been infected and later cleared ended up testing positively once again. The problem was far from over. No one answered the questions: are the tests accurate? Can a person be "reinfected"? Can this happen with the same strain of virus? Has the virus changed a tad? Has it changed a lot? Has it changed for the better or for worse? What we do know is that these same questions and these same problems were seen in domestic animals previously. We have a lot to learn about the corona family.

In the latter part of April, the government started lifting restrictions.

In May, after a period of control, a new cluster of cases emerged in South Korea with an index case involving nightclubbing. This was very active nightclubbing with over a thousand contacts. There were some aspects of the nightclubbing which raised eyebrows and divided opinion as to confidentiality. It was a question of preferred sexual activity which was felt to be private. Here, the health of the public prevailed and the government once again took charge..

As I finish this paper, the virus is not finished. I have indicated how it affected us after it first was recognized in South Korea and the United States. I followed it for a few months. From this, you can see that even when it looks like there is control, it takes only one person to start it all over again.

As I read the current figures while ending this paper, I realize that the virus is not the same in each place that it strikes, and I realize that each place where the virus strikes has had a different response. Even now, the virus is surging in some places while declining in others.

To make a fairer comparison, while realizing that we have many variables, we can cite death rates per million cases. Even if premature, these were all taken at the same time by a single source. They are obviously going to change, but we are comparing countries at the same point in time. True, the identification of cases and the attribution of death from the virus will vary from country to country. Nonetheless, these figures give us food for thought and a means to compare how each country has been struck and how each has responded to the pandemic.

Deaths per million cases:

Taiwan	0.3
Singapore	3.2
Japan	4.7
S Korea	4.9
Canada	6.9
Germany	93.9
USA	233
UK	480

By looking at South Korea, you see that she did well in spite of a major second and third wave. Other countries with a similar strategy of test, trace, and isolate have generally done well.

South Korea is considered to have one of the most exemplary of public health programs in dealing with COVID-19. Taiwan, Singapore, and Vietnam have similar programs.

I respectfully thank those who read this paper. I wish the best and pray for recovery to those who are struck by this Coronavirus plague, and I give deep appreciation to my uncle who has fought in all three of these coronavirus battles. I apologize for any inaccuracy in reproducing material from his detailed notes. I thank him for hammering all the information into my brain. Some of it took more than one blow to register.

The list of references follows.

We have not included Kim's list of references here. Many of them came by way of his uncle, others though Kim's late night searches on the computer, and a few through the kindness of his sister – or his friend, Acacia.

AFTERWORD

Months later, returning to the town where the Sappiance family had resided, one could find information and misinformation. There was no shortage of stories. These were muffled and muttered behind masks, uttered six to ten feet away, and, while not consistent, stated with authority. That which follows appears to have some degree of authenticity.

The public school had not crystallized its plan for fall reopening. Those who were responsible had many contingency plans. They wanted neither to be the first nor the last, but to be safe and exemplary. They were still reeling from the tragic accident. They had no desire to add to that grief. This was their opportunity to be a leader in an area other than sports; they insisted that they should be a leader in how to reopen.

The first need was to replace the school nurse who had moved out of the area. Many stressed the critical importance of this individual in supervising activities, ensuring distancing and masking, and coordinating efforts with other departments. The nurse should be there to test students, and be ready to supervise administering a vaccine when available.

The PTA had indicated the desire to continue a school lunch program, but to have it meticulously prepared, individually boxed, and consumed in well separated places since masks would be forsaken at that time.

They sought someone whom the students would want to seek out rather than avoid, a counsellor and confidant. The nurse should be an educational leader employing preventative measures.

They had plans for desk separations, room ventilation, UV light sources, hand wipe stations, and extra sinks for hand washing. They wanted to do this right. Ventilation and spacing were to be considered gold standards and masks were to be mandatory.

Naturally, politics, taxes, and hammering costs brought the board of select people into the fray. They looked to other towns for methods to copy. They developed mottoes, even copying those from a century past – recalling the Great Epidemic of 1918. One was, "We want education within walls, but not to sicken the student." So it was that 1918 morphed into 2020.

Complications arose when the local secondary school was designated to be a reserve "pack hospital," ie, a building suited for and fitted with hospital equipment in packaged form, to be activated in the event of a mass disaster.

The most anticipated mass disaster was another wave of the virus. Certain areas of the school were then "off limits" so as to be free of disruption or possible contamination.

There was a nurse practitioner who had recently graduated and was getting further training with a specialist in infectious diseases; the specialist already had a PA, two nurses, and a nurse practitioner, so this was a fortuitous opportunity for all. He would even have the periodic backup of his last mentor. Hiring this man and combining him with the nurse would divide responsibilities. That both eased and accelerated the quest for filling of the role considered by many to be most important for re-opening of schools in 1918, but altered to fit the needs of a century later. It was the 1918 school nurse morphed into two complementary bodies, and with back up from the director of health and an epidemiologist. Now to find the money to fund this. That opened another floodgate of currents and counter currents.

Folks associated with the public school were still arguing over the auto accident, some denying that the vast majority of the dozen beer cans being empty reflected drinking while driving. Others took solace in the relatively minimal injuries incurred by the older couple in the other, sideswiped car – although some would say that she, the elderly passenger in that unfortunate car, now being relegated to a wheelchair was far from minor. A memorial plaque had been placed in the gym, noting Thomas Brandos as having been an outstanding athlete, succumbing before finishing his senior year. No plaque was raised for *his* passenger, Mandy. They had a joint funeral with a procession of cars circling the school for an hour, complying with local COVID regulations.

Initially, a crucial shortage of tests in the States was gradually corrected – only to be replaced by tests too often deemed faulted. Individual antigen tests failed to live up to promised sensitivities and screening tests received even more criticism. Antibody tests were similarly troubled. Only one thing remained certain, COVID-19 was still a clinical diagnosis.

Economies opened in diverse degrees. Some had definitive plans, others had no apparent theme. Mask requirements were lifted when temperatures rose in one school in Isreal, only to see a sudden and sorry explosion of new COVID cases as a result. A few schools opened in the States, but then closed a few days later, due to positive testing of student and/or faculty.

Kim and Barbara were said to have moved, but no one knew quite where. Some said that Kim had a scholarship in a Canadian school. His paper had been well received in that country, and the Canadian model was much like the South Korean. Still others said that crossing the border was extremely difficult and unlikely to have happened.

A few insisted that Barbara was with Kim, wherever she was, but others were equally adamant that she was now alone, at some university where she supplemented her cost by teaching taekwondo.

Work on a vaccine had progressed at what was considered by some to be warp speed. There were over 200 potential candidates. A great variety of contenders were being developed by an equal diversity of companies from around the globe, not a few of them working cooperatively.

Whole virus vaccines using altered, non-replicating adenoviruses to mimic the crucial features of the coronavirus were early contenders. These had the advantage of previous use with Ebola and acted by actually "infecting" the body and generating an immune reaction across the spectrum of antibody and T-cell. However, those people with previous adenovirus infection would be expected to knock out this new "threat" before the critical add on corona features could do their job. Many young folks would already have adenoviral antibodies which would diminish or mute the response.

Whereas RNA based vaccines had never been successful in the past, even they were touted, pushed, and showed good early results. These relied upon a messenger RNA which would instruct cells of the recipient to make spike proteins which would then be seen as foreign and invoke an antibody response. People rushed to be volunteers in phase III trials.

Attenuated viruses and Inactivated viruses were being produced in India. Less conventional methods held promise with recombinant viral sub-units aimed at "spike proteins." Particular families of animals were recognized as having a special ability to produce not one, but two major kinds of antibodies, the second group being a nano antibody. While sharks did this, they promised to be poor candidates for the laboratory; on the other hand, camelids, like the llama and alpaca, provided a means of investigating this further.

Lurking behind this were the risks of the coronavirus changing so as to elude the vaccine makers effort, combining with other viruses and presenting further problems, and even doing as dengue and the respiratory syncytial virus had done, wherein vaccine ended up ironically enhancing the virus (antibody dependent enhancement or ADE).

Countries rushed to be first and foremost. Companies invested hundreds of millions of dollars in manufacturing of viruses under the most stringent conditions well before they had shown adequate success to warrant such production.

Indeed, some countries with a less than enviable reputation for their action in the past appeared to be cutting corners. Yet, in this race to find a vaccine, the emphasis evidently was how to produce a vaccine that would protect the inoculated from being severely ill, not in how to prevent the recipient from contracting the disease; the latter concept would address the problem of those being vaccine-protected not being possible spreaders.

Mrs. Sappiance was, up at all hours and asleep at all hours. She was continuing media-class teaching around the globe, setting the alarm for France, Singapore, Brazil, and Chile in order to have her student-teacher conferences. Her cooking somewhat suffered as a result.

She worried, as she always had. She worried about the risks of school re-opening to campus teaching, she worried about it not re-opening to campus teaching, she worried about her Korean surrogate children, and she naturally worried about her own children. She knew where Barbara was, but when asked, simply replied, "She's very well settled and safe … healthy and happy." Then she would smile but say no more.

Benji and Acacia got jobs. They were hired by the prep school to label each tree, develop a course where students would learn not only different species, but botany basics, forestry associations, cultivation, and even paleobotany. This would be a first, a student-teacher collaboration. They did this while trying to catch Mrs Sappiance during some of her waking moments – and while not in the kitchen. They hoped that the school would re-open so that they might carry this on at safe outside distancing. Nonetheless, they did have a backup plan.

How she got there, and by bending what regulations, there seemed to be no agreement, but Hyo-joo Park was back in South Korea and she had graduated, She was reported as having been at the side of her dear uncle, "Samchon." Tirelessly assisting him, whether in his research to further clarify this coronavirus scourge, caring for patients, or arguing with authorities about premature openings of the "economy" at the risk of illness or death, she was there. The South Korean economy had suffered greatly and Hyo-joo no longer looked forward to opening the mail or reading emails – unless from a reliable and known source; she had received too many threats from those with opposing views. Awaiting her return to formal schooling, she considered herself to be learning still more in her long hours of assisting Samchon. She had been accepted into an accelerated program combining college with medical school, but that was yet to materialize due to health restrictions.

Samchon wrote a noteworthy paper on the coronavirus family. Hyo-joo had been at his side in the research, and found herself doing the final editing. In this, Samchon gave great credit to others from a wide variety of countries. In the UK, they had noted a half dozen, distinctly different presentations of COVID-19. Samchon added over a dozen more. The UK paper had separated the types into two flu-like presentations, one with and one without fever, one GI presentation, and then three severe forms. Each of these had anosmia, a loss of smell. All but one had chest pain.

Samchon, before adding to the list, elaborated on the UK observations, taking information from other doctors around the world. He pointed out that it was the character of the chest pain, a persistent and severe *pressure*, like that of a heart attack that was noteworthy; indeed, it was often persistent for weeks while in the absence of any EKG abnormality. Similarly, the UK study had noted fatigue, but Samchon elaborated, indicating that this was sometimes profound, possibly resulting in a person crawling rather than walking. Whereas the UK study had indicated diarrhea in one of the severe forms as well as the GI form, Samchon underscored the often forgotten other symptoms of GI upset, including nausea, abdominal distress, vomiting and diarrhea; he stressed how the diarrhea, as in piglets and cattle, could be explosive (and, consequently being far more contagious through aerosolization); he also stressed a premonitory GI upset of varying degree – only to be followed by the more impressive respiratory syndrome. He emphasized that progressive shortness of breath was a dire finding deserving aggressive response.

Then he *added* to the list, not just from his own experience, but from those in other countries, countries where the proclivity of the virus to change, to give entirely different presentations – illustrated just how difficult a foe this one was to characterize. There was, of course, the barely symptomatic group and asymptomatic group: those with no notable symptoms, yet, upon dogged questioning, sometimes unearthed forgotten or minor symptoms. There was the "pink eye" group with a conjunctivitis, possibly a singular finding and presumably infectious. Other minimally symptomatic patients included the mildly upset stomach with a change in bowel habits, those with a passing sore throat, mild head ache, or just not up to par.

Then there were the odd balls. There was the argument over rashes on the skin or on mucous membranes. There were cases that seemed to be a variant of "Kawasaki's disease" and those deemed to be an alternant to Pernio (or chilblains). These appeared to be further variations of the coronavirus, the latter a more localized reflection of the virus tagging on to the lining of blood vessels.

In more severe forms, this was seen as an ironic and dangerous dissemi-nated intravascular coagulation, and raised a flag as to anti-coagulation as part of treatment. This was impressive enough to some, particularly in certain geo-graphic areas, that they voiced a recommendation to anticoagulant *all* seriously ill patients.

There was not just the virus, but the host, of course. A well meaning, but blatantly excessive reaction of the body pouring out and burning up the reserve of inflammatory response: *a cytokine storm* – offered a very different and most severe form of presentation.

Hyo-joo found this work fascinating. She was a sponge to every challenge. She loved the combining of historical, veterinary, and current research and ideas. Gradually, she could anticipate some of his next moves, and when she did this, a subtle smile dame to Samchon's countenance. She was torn between the com-passion for the poor victims and the fascination of unraveling of the problems.

The amazing prevalence of not just confusion, but of many other neurological findings in both early presentation and persistence afterward was especially note-worthy to Samchon. These ranged from mild and ephemeral mental changes to dementia, partial paralyses and seizures. It recalled Samchon's earlier experience with SARS1 and MERS. He saw these as grim forebodings, too often neglected.

There were the expected, the predictable presentations of course, The ACE2 receptors in the throat and upper respiratory tract explained the sore throat and cold-like presentations in many. Those same receptors in the heart justified the general inflammation of the heart, or cardiomyopathy, along with heart attacks, abnormal rhythms, and blocks of the electrical circuitry. Now, his colleagues were suggesting that those same receptors were present in the supporting cells of the nervous system and helped to explain some of the neurological complications.

Hyo-joo had allied her uncle with a veterinarian, much to the delight of each. ACE2 receptors in the liver, kidney, and reproductive organs were known, but find-ing the virus in the semen was of further concern. She and the veterinarian were still searching for cases of hemorrhagic diarrhea since this was so remarkable in cattle and piglets. This quest, along with many other important clues worth follow-ing, finally fell – as did the progenitor.

It was with the help of the veterinarian that Hyo-joo was able to finish Samchon's paper – arguably incomplete or premature. Samchon's last days went quickly and ironically, succumbing to the corona family that he had repeatedly battled so determinedly. Hyo-joo's letter to Kim was marred by tears.

Acknowledgements

This book was written in order to share the turmoil and truth of the first few months of the third charge of the coronavirus horde.

The Afterword indicates some of the major changes that occurred between the finishing of the novella and the final version being sent for publication.

While many people have have been kind enough to read various preliminary renditions of this novella, some have been especially instrumental in helping me take a critical history of the virus and incorporating it into a story.

My daughters, Lynette, Heather, and Roxanne have patiently labored over changing concepts, precise wording, and each illustration; their help has been immeasurable and without them, the book would still be floating around in my mind. They never complained and always did more than asked. Patiently, they corrected my atrocious spelling. They facilitated the morphing of the book from *pages* to *word* and artfully and appropriately scanned my sketches.

My daughter Jenna, herself an exquisite artist, has guided my hand from afar. My wife, Helen has listened to me voice the pros and cons of various presentations; her patience, judgement, and wisdom are most appreciated.

Many dear friends, knowledgeable in the medical and scientific fields, have waded through various stages of the book. Dr. Kim Manwaring, a neurosurgeon, has been astutely analytical. His guidance has reflected the need to search for the positive and to focus on different generations. Dr. Albert Pizzo has been a constant source of encouragement. Dr. Richard Dibala has offered candid and helpful suggestions. Dr. Kendra Gorlitsky has been a faithful fan from afar. Dr. C., herself a victim of COVID, has been a fan and continued commentator. Dr. Susan Diaz has emphasized the connection with young adults.

Others have kindly read and commented on the text, yielded opinions on the artwork, and given realistic analyses that have been taken to heart. I thank them: Sue, Margo, Jocelyn, Joyce, and more – thank you.

The illustrations have been provided by the same artist that has kindly done work for my previous books. He doesn't charge and doesn't ask for recognition. That notwithstanding, he is very sensitive, so I ask that any criticism of his work be couched in gentle terms.